PAUL DANIELS'
MAGIC
SHOWCASE

PAUL DANIELS' MAGIC SHOWCASE

PAUL DANIELS'
MAGIC SHOWCASE

PAUL DANIELS
&
BARRY MURRAY

BBC BOOKS

FOR S.A.M., F.C.M. AND M.L.M. ... GREATER MAGIC

Published by BBC Books,
a division of BBC Enterprises Limited,
Woodlands, 80 Wood Lane
London W12 0TT
First published 1992
© Paul Daniels and Barry Murray 1992
ISBN 0 563 36352 5
Designed by Roger Daniels
Photographs by Matthew May
Illustrations by Dennis Patten
Set in Gill and Monotype Script by
Butler & Tanner Ltd, Frome, Somerset
Printed and bound in Great Britain by
Butler & Tanner Ltd, Frome, Somerset
Cover printed in England by Richard Clay Ltd., St Ives PLC

Contents

Introduction

Hi, this is Paul Daniels speaking, welcome to my world of magic. If you are interested in magic, you have come to the right book. In between these covers you will find sixty-seven (count them) terrific tricks that are easy to learn, easy to do and require virtually no preparation. If you show some of these tricks to your friends, you'll have more fun than you would ever have thought possible. However, just like learning to ride a bike or swim like a fish, you have to take it one step at a time. There are some tricks in this book that you can do the very first time you try them; others need a little practice before you show them to anyone, so don't forget to practise.

The chapters have been laid out to suit the average day of the school person that you are. There are tricks that can be done over breakfast, in the classroom or the playground. Tricks you can pull from your pockets at any time, tricks that everyone can try at a party, even tricks to baffle grown-ups!

So, really, you have no excuse for not being able to perform some first-class magic, any time, anywhere.

But, you will remember to practise, won't you?

Say, 'Yes, Paul'!

Good.

Bye for now.

a
Brief History of Mystery

Magic is as old as mankind – that much we can be sure of. What we will never know is the name of the first person who set out to amaze and entertain his fellow man. Thus, even from the very beginning, there is mystery in the history of magic.

A hieroglyph on the wall of a tomb in Beni Hassan, Egypt, which experts claim shows a demonstration of the Cups and Balls trick, was painted some 2500 years before the birth of Christ. So, over 5000 years ago, recorded history shows there was magic in the world. The Westcar Papyrus, written around 1700 BC (now in the Bode Museum in Berlin, Germany), records the wondrous feats of Dedi of Dedsnefru who, when called to appear before the famous Cheops, King of Kings and builder of the Great Pyramid at Gizeh, delighted and baffled the great king by chopping off the heads of live animals and putting them back on again, restoring them to normal life. We would love to see these feats as performed by Dedi today, not because we don't believe them to be possible – why, we decapitated and restored Debbie McGee's head just the other week on national television – but because we would like to see the manner, the style and presentation that Dedi used to stage his magic. The recorded history of magic is all about performing magicians and classic effects.

The Cups and Balls trick was described by the

Spaniard, Seneca the Younger born in 3 BC, and by Alciphran of Athens in approximately AD 250. The trick pops up in drawings, paintings and woodcuts by artists throughout the Middle Ages.

The first time secrets of magic appeared in print was a section on conjuring in *The Discoverie of Witchcraft* by Reginald Scot, published in 1584. That was during the reign of Queen Elizabeth I.

By the seventeenth century magicians' names were familiar to many people. As famous for their physical oddities as for their magical skills, they performed in taverns and markets and fairs. Some made a rich living; Issac Fawkes, a noted fairground magician, was purported to have left £10,000 when he died in 1731, a tremendous sum for the time! What stories must have been told, what performers, what curiosities — performers who ate stones, learned pigs that were presented as understanding reading and could do arithmetic, men who could spout jets of water from their mouths, such wonders!

Gradually, magical performers became more accomplished, their performances more complete. They demonstrated their art in society salons and they trod the boards of theatres throughout Europe.

The arrival of a giant among magicians heralded the dawn of modern magic. In Paris, France, on 3 July 1845, a former watchmaker and mechanic, Jean-Eugène Robert-

Houdin, opened a theatre of magic. He was the first to present magic in the style that, today, we would consider modern. He was a prolific inventor and wrote books that are still rich in magic creativity. He became the father of modern magic.

In the early 1890s a young, and deeply ambitious magician named Erich Weiss took Houdin's name and simply added the letter 'i' on the end to become Houdini. He became, arguably, the most famous magician who ever lived. He operated during the golden time of magic when magicians were superstars. They often toured with tons of equipment, particularly in America where names like Keller and Thurston dominated the magic world.

In England in 1873 two men, John Nevil Maskelyne and his partner George Cooke, opened a specialist magical theatre in Piccadilly, London, called the Egyptian Hall; elsewhere, magic thrived in the music-halls.

In more recent times the advent of television hastened the disappearance of the halls and gave birth to a new generation of magicians: David Nixon, Tommy Cooper and, of course, Paul Daniels.

How will magic progress from here? Nobody knows, but, if magic has been around as long as man, then it is logical to assume that magic will be around as long as there is man.

You Can Do Magic

*N*ow that you have gained a little knowledge about the fascinating history of magic, it is time for you to take your first step along the yellow brick road to becoming a magician. You will need a pack of cards, a banana, one needle (be careful with this), a pencil and paper, and your own left and right hands!

I Can See through Me

This trick is probably the most important trick you will ever do in your entire life. Why? Because, my little magical person, it is the very first trick I am going to teach you.

Effect

It is nothing very ambitious as tricks go, just how to see right through the palm of your left hand!

SECRET

Roll up a piece of paper, or a comic, or magazine, into a tube and hold it to your right eye so you can look through it like a telescope. Now hold your left hand flat, with palm up towards you at eye level, and put the left edge of your hand, just below the bottom of your little finger, against the far end of the tube. Now for the magic. Keeping both eyes open, slowly move your

left hand towards your face and you will clearly be able to see right through the centre of your left palm. If you look at the photograph of me doing it you will be able to see me through your hand, looking at you looking at me! This is all very unusual, but then that is how it's supposed to be in this strange magic business. I wonder if you can figure out what makes the effect happen?

The Magic Banana

Not only is this an unusual and surprising trick, it must be one of the few tricks you can eat when you've performed it!

EFFECT

The magician asks members of his audience to call out several numbers from one to ten. As each number is called out, it is written on a small piece of paper which the magician folds up into a small square and drops into a glass or a bowl. When seven different numbers have been called, written down on small pieces of paper, folded and dropped into the glass, the magician invites a spectator to come forward, dip his fingers into the glass and remove one piece of paper. Then he is to open it and read out loud the number written on it. He does so and calls out the number 'four'.

The magician then draws everybody's attention to a banana on a plate on the table. He picks it up and peels the banana which is found to be already magically sliced into four pieces.

SECRET

The banana has been secretly prepared in advance by carefully (mind your fingers) inserting a needle into the banana and gently twisting the banana so that, in effect, you are slicing the banana inside its skin. Do this

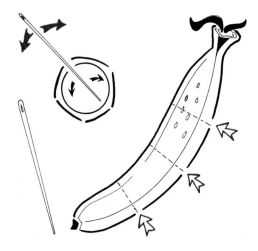

in three different places. If you insert the needle in dark parts of the banana skin the holes won't show. What is really sneaky about this trick is that the number four is forced. As each number is called out, instead of writing that number you actually write the number four each time, so you end up with seven number fours on the pieces of paper. But you must pretend it is their number you are writing, so don't make your deception obvious.

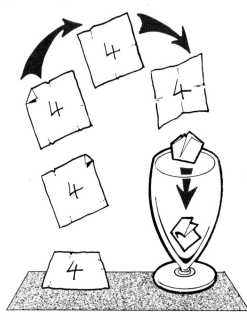

Spectator Cuts the Aces

Effect

The magician, that's you, shuffles a pack of cards. Then, placing the pack on a table, he asks a spectator to cut off three-quarters of the pack and place it down to the right, next to the quarter pack left on the table. Then, from the larger portion, he cuts off two-thirds and places it down to the right, and then he must cut this last portion in half and place it down to the right of the other cards. There will now be four face-down stacks of cards in a row on the table.

Now, starting from the left, the spectator picks up the cards that were originally the bottom portion of the pack. He then moves three cards from the top to the bottom of that portion. He deals from the cards he is already holding, one card on to each of the other three piles on the table. This is then repeated in turn with each of the other three piles of cards. He picks up the second stack of cards and deals one card on to each of the three piles on the table. This is repeated with the third stack, then the fourth.

When the spectator has completed this dealing process, the magician (that's still you) says the magic word – **ABRACADABRA**. You tell the spectator to turn over the top card of each packet and, wonder of wonders, he turns up an Ace on top of each pile.

SECRET

Secretly (this means out of the spectator's sight) put the four Aces together on top of the pack before you begin to shuffle. Then false shuffle the pack, keeping the four Aces on top. You can do this either by overhand shuffling and simply not shuffling as far as

the top cards, or by riffle shuffling – cut the pack in half and with your thumbs riffle the two halves together but retain the top cards (the four Aces) with your right thumb so that they remain on top after shuffling and squaring the pack. Now, hand the pack to the spectator and have him go through the cutting and dealing procedure (as in Effect). You will find that, if he follows your instructions, the four Aces will automatically end up on top of each pile.

This is a very good trick. Keep the secret to yourself, don't tell anybody how it's done.

The Mixed-up Card Trick

Try this on yourself first, then you can try it on your friends. You can even do it over the telephone!

EFFECT

All good magicians should be able to spell properly. You can interpret that word 'spell' two ways if you think about it; this trick combines both.

SECRET

Pick up your pack of cards. Deal three cards in a face-down pile on the table. Cut the cards in your hands. Deal three more cards on top of those on the table, then cut the cards in your hands again. Deal three more on to those on the table and cut the cards in your hands. Deal two cards on to those on the table.

Now, look at and *remember* the last card you dealt before returning it face down on to those on the table; put the rest of the pack on the pile of cards on the table. Pick up the pack, *double* the number of spots on your card (remember an Ace counts as 1, and so on; for the picture cards a Jack = 11, a Queen = 12 and a King 13). Deal that many cards in a pile on the table. Turn the cards in your hand face up and put them on to the cards on the table. Pick them all up.

Deal twenty cards if your card was a Heart or a Spade or deal twenty-four cards if a Club or a Diamond. Turn the cards in your hand face up and place on the cards on the table. Pick them all up. Deal thirteen cards if your card was red or eighteen if it was a black card. Turn the cards face up in your hand, put them on the pile on the table. Pick up all the cards.

Now deal one card for each letter of Paul's name: **PAUL DANIELS**. The card that falls on the last letter will be the chosen card.

A *Real Old Timer*

This trick has probably been around as long as there has been magic with playing cards. The reason why it has lasted for such a long time is that it is a very good trick.

*E*FFECT

The magician deals three rows of cards, face up on the table. The spectator thinks of one of the cards and the magician successfully names the thought-of card.

*S*ECRET

Deal three cards, face up, from left to right in a row next to each other, then deal another three face up on top of them, but so you can still see part of their faces. Continue dealing three cards at a time in this fashion until you have three rows with seven cards in each row (see *photo 1*).

Ask a spectator to think of one of the cards on the table. Then, without telling

you the name of his card, he indicates the row which contains the card he is thinking of. You then gather up the cards, one row at a time, without altering the position of any of the cards. Make sure that the row containing his selected card is the second row you pick up. This will place the row containing his card between the other two in your hand (see *photo 2*).

Turn the cards face down in your hand and then deal out three more rows of seven cards, face up as you did before. Ask the spectator to indicate which row now contains the card he is thinking of. Pick up the cards, again making sure that you place the row containing his card between the other two.

Turn the packet of cards face down in your hand and then deal out three more rows of seven cards, face up as you did before. Ask the spectator to indicate which row his card is in. At this point casually look at the fourth card in the row he indicated; this will be the card he is thinking of (see *photo 3*).

Now we use a little of what magicians call showmanship, to make the effect more exciting. Gather up all the cards and spread them between your hands so only you can see their faces. Ask the spectator to concentrate on the card he is thinking of. Take his selected card and place it face down on the table (see *photo 4*). Ask him for the first time to name the card he is thinking of. When he does so, tell him to turn over the card on the table (see *photo 5*). It is his card!

If you are asked to repeat the trick, why not perform a different version, 'The Lazy Magician' on page 57? It'll make you seem an even greater magician!

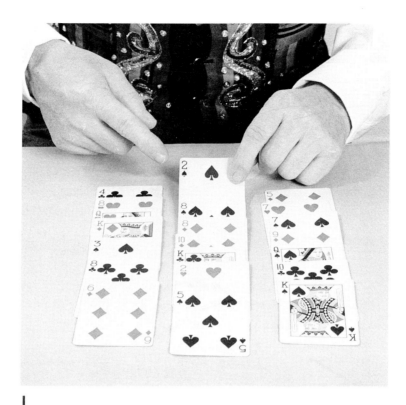

1

2

3

4

5

$\mathcal{M}$AGICIANS' CODE

As you are now on your way to becoming a magician it is most important that you remember these three golden rules:

1 *Practice Makes Perfect* Don't just learn a trick but practise it until you can do it almost without having to think about it. That way you will be a credit to magic.

2 *Be Entertaining* Dress your tricks with interesting or funny patter.

3 *Keep the Secret to Yourself* Never tell anyone how it's done. If you once give away the secret of a trick then it will no longer be a source of pleasure to your audience or a secret for you. People love magic and its mysteries; treasure its secrets well.

Magic
in the Morning

Good morning, good morning, what a wonderful day for a magic trick or two, or three, or four, or more. So let us head for the kitchen to discover what tricks we can do over breakfast.

Nosey

All you need for this strange effect is a spoon; a teaspoon or a tablespoon will do equally well.

*E*FFECT

The early morning magician (that's you) takes a spoon and, putting the bowl of the spoon on to his nose, slowly takes his hand away, leaving the spoon hanging there.

*S*ECRET

It sounds easy enough to do and for some it is. (One tip is to breathe on to the bowl of the spoon.) Others will have to experiment as it is an acquired knack. Trial, error and perseverance, the three vital ingredients of any success story, may need to be applied here. But, once you have the knack, it's yours forever. So practise, that's the secret, not only of this trick, but of all tricks. It's a very amusing effect to try with your friends, so do try it.

Half a Dozen Eggs

Make sure you have Mum's permission before you attempt the following funny stunts:

1 How to tell a hard-boiled egg from an unboiled egg. Try spinning the egg on its side. Hard-boiled eggs are easy to spin, unboiled aren't.

2 Spin an unboiled egg on its side; put your finger lightly on top to stop it, then the split second it stops take your finger off and the egg will start spinning again. The continued movement of the contents causes this.

3 Did you know that, if you wrap a piece of string around an egg and try to burn it, it won't. The egg actually absorbs the heat. Make sure that Mum or Dad supervise this.

4 A great challenge for Dad is to say that you can put an unboiled egg on a piece of newspaper in such a way that he can't kick it off with his foot. The secret is to put the newspaper halfway under a closed door with the egg on one side and Dad on the other.

5 Here's another great challenge for Dad, or a friend. Tell him to clasp his hands together with fingers interlocked, then you put an unboiled egg between his palms so the two ends of the egg are touching the centre of each palm. Now challenge him to break the egg by squeezing his palms together (but make sure the egg isn't cracked). He won't be able to, it's impossible.

6 The following effect should only be done with Mum's or Dad's help because it involves matches, and we all know how dangerous they can be. Take a hard-boiled egg and carefully remove the shell. Now put some loosely scrumpled paper inside a perfectly dry milk bottle. Have Dad light a match and drop it into the milk bottle so it sets the paper alight. Directly the paper has caught fire, press the point of the egg firmly into the mouth of the bottle and hold it there. After a few seconds the burning paper will go out and you can take your hand away from the egg. Now watch very carefully and you will see the egg squeeze itself right into the bottle!

When the bottle has cooled run some water into it under the kitchen tap to remove the burnt paper and matchstick.

Pour the water out, poking the egg back

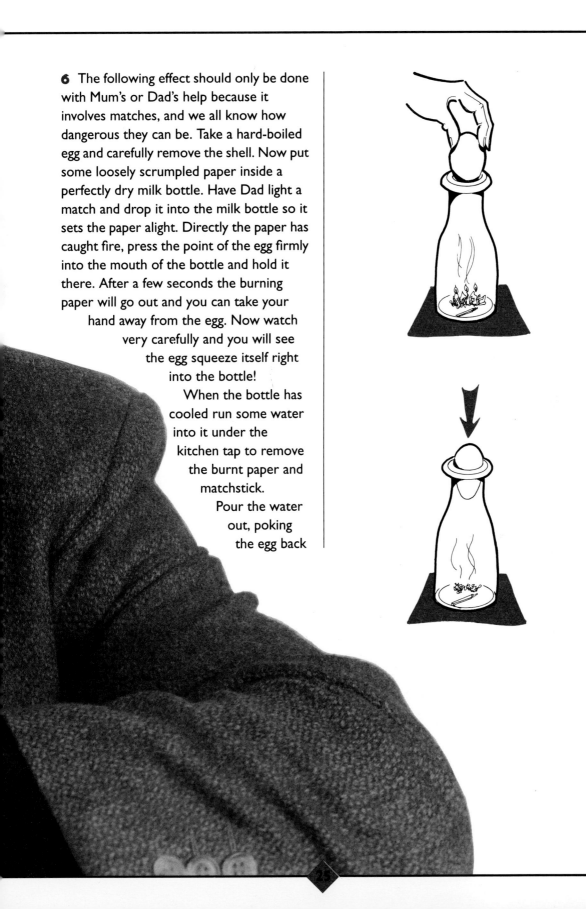

up inside the bottle to facilitate this and leave it overnight to dry out. You will be left with a very unusual 'funnyosity' to show your friends.

To remove the egg, turn the bottle upside down so the egg rolls into the neck of the bottle, then blow very hard into the bottle,

take your mouth off the bottle and keep holding it upside down. Get ready to catch the egg as it squeezes itself out of the bottle.

I wonder if you can figure out what scientific principle makes both effects work. Ask your schoolteacher if Mum and Dad aren't sure.

How Else?

EFFECT

Tie a length of string to the handle of a cup or mug. Ask a friend to lift the cup into the air by the end of the string; now hand him a pair of scissors. The challenge is for him to cut the string near the middle of its length without letting the cup drop. There are two conditions. He can't touch the cup or let it rest on anything, and he can't hold the string beneath the point at which he cuts it.

SECRET

Wind the end of the string around one finger. Make some slack in the middle of the length of string, gather it up, make a loop and tie it into a tight knot. Take the scissors, remind him of the conditions of the challenge, and cut the loop of the knot and you've done it. How else?

One of the great classic tricks of magic is the Cups and Balls. It is also one of the oldest documented magic tricks. All the greatest magicians have mastered the skilled sleight of hand necessary to perform the effect perfectly. We have performed various cup-and-ball routines over the years and Paul's one-cup, one-ball presentation has become famous amongst magicians and the public.

Cups and Sponges

Here is a much simplified version of the cups and balls that doesn't require sleight of hand. It does need practice to master the routine, but this wonderful trick is worth all the practice you have in you.

Effect

Using three empty yogurt cups and three small sponge cubes you perform a bewildering series of vanishes, reappearances and penetrations.

Secret

The reason this is such a baffling trick to non-magicians is the use of a clever magical principle: the secret use of four sponge cubes although spectators only ever see three sponge cubes. This enables you to be one or more moves ahead of the spectators. You will also require a magic wand; at breakfast a tablespoon is most appropriate. The four small sponges can be cut from an old bath sponge; try to make

them similar in shape and size. Try to get plastic yogurt tubs that have a recessed bottom and are all the same flavour, so each cup looks the same as the others.

Follow the diagrams as you go. We have labelled the cups A, B and C and suggest you do the same while learning the routine.

1 Start with the three cups mouth upwards in a stack. A is the bottom cup. B, which has a sponge hidden in it, is in the middle and C is the top cup. The three sponges are on the table to the right.

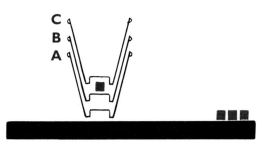

2 Pick up the stack of cups with your left hand; with your right hand take the bottom cup (A) with your thumb to the right, remove it from the stack, turn it straight

over and put it on the table, mouth down, to the right.

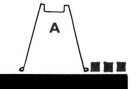

3 Repeat the same sequence of moves with cup B and place it mouth down in front of you. Just do this smartly, turning the cup

over, mouth downwards, near the table top and the sponge will stay hidden. This is the way you always turn the cups over when placing them down on the table, making sure you keep the mouths of the cups turned towards your body and turning the cups in the same way and same speed each time – so nothing will ever look suspicious.

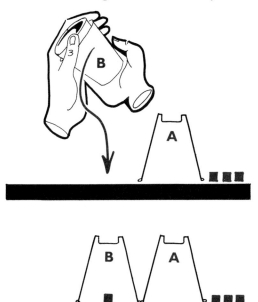

4 Take the third cup (C) from your left hand and turn it face down on the table to the left, exactly as you did the others. The

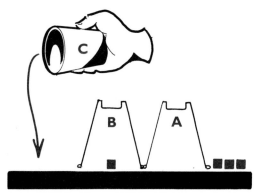

spectators will think there are three empty cups face down on the table; we know, however, that there is a sponge hidden under the middle cup (B).

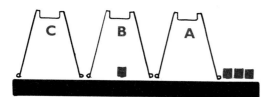

5 Take one of the three visible sponges and put it on top of the centre cup (B). Now

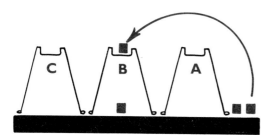

put cup A on cup B, then put cup C on cup A, so that all three are stacked mouth downwards.

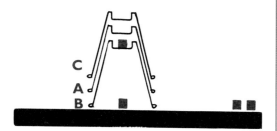

Pick up your magic spoon, tap the top cup, say the magic word

ALAMALAGOOLA

(now that's what you call a magic word).

Lift the stack of cups with your right hand to reveal the previously hidden sponge which has apparently penetrated cup B. As the sponge is revealed place the stack mouth upwards into your left hand.

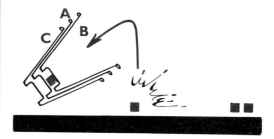

6 Leave the sponge on the table and repeat the same turning-over, putting-down moves as before. Take, turn over, and place the bottom cup (C) to the right of the sponge on the table. The next cup (A), with hidden sponge in it, place down and over the visible sponge, which has just been revealed. Place the third cup (B) to the left of cup A.

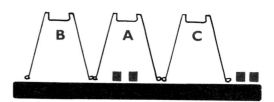

The set-up is, as you look at it, cup B to the left, cup A (with two sponges under it) in the middle, and cup C to the right. The spectators think there is only one sponge under cup A, but you are one move ahead of them as there are really two sponges under cup A.

7 Now pick up another visible sponge from the table and put it on top of the centre cup (A).

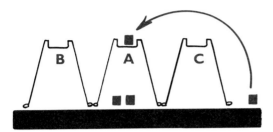

Place cup C over cup A and cup B over cup C.

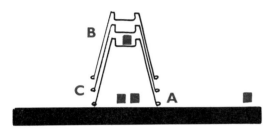

Pick up your magic spoon, give the stack two taps, one hot, one cold, say

ALAMALAGOOLA

and lift the stack with your right hand, turning the cups over and putting them mouth upwards into your left hand. As this happens all attention is on the revelation of two sponges on the table; another penetration has taken place.

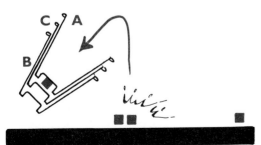

8 Repeat the same set of moves as before. Place cup B mouth down to the right, cup C in the middle over the two visible sponges (secretly adding the hidden sponge), and cup A to the left.

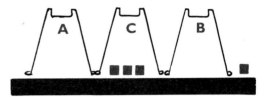

9 Pick up the last sponge (the third sponge as far as the spectators are concerned) and put it on top of cup C, followed by cup A on cup B.

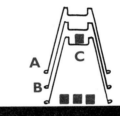

Pick up the magic spoon, say the magic word, lift up the stack, turn it over as you put the stack into the left hand as all attention (including yours) is on the three sponges on the table.

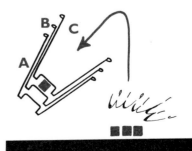

10 You are now back to the set-up with which you started the routine. Three sponges are visible on the table, three cups are stacked mouth upwards in your left hand, with the fourth sponge hidden in the middle cup (B).

11 To finish the trick take cup A and put it face down to the left. Take cup B, with the hidden sponge, and put it face down to the right and, finally, put cup C in the middle. All the cups are behind, not covering, the three visible sponges.

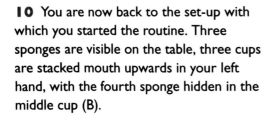

Pick up one sponge and put it on top of cup A. Put cup C on top of cup A. Pick up the

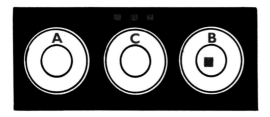

magic spoon and say the magic words,

FISH AND CHIPS,

and lift cups A and C straight up off the table (don't turn them over) with your left

hand to reveal – nothing! With your right hand lift up cup B to show that the sponge has apparently travelled across from cup A.

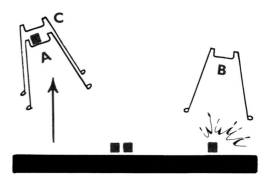

12 To clean up the trick, turn your left hand over so that the cups A and C are mouth up, put cup B into cup A, pick up the three visible sponges and drop them into cup B, add the magic spoon and put everything away out of sight.

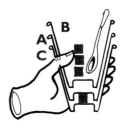

Practise until you can perform the routine smoothly (doing it in front of a mirror will help), almost without thinking, and you will have mastered a classic of magic.

Magic at School

apart from the fun of school work, and it should be fun considering that every day, in every way you are becoming a little more knowledgeable in a wonderful variety of subjects, the classroom is a rich source of potential magic props. Step into my conjuring masterclass and I shall further your magical education.

Once Bitten

This is a cheeky challenge-type stunt to play on a friend.

Effect

Ask a friend to bite an inch from the end of your ruler. He'll probably think you're crazy until you show him how.

Secret

Hold one end of your ruler an inch away from your mouth then ... bite!

It's not absolutely necessary to be crazy to be a magician, but some people think it helps!

$\mathcal{A}$s a Rule

All you need for this interesting little puzzler is a ruler.

$\mathcal{E}$FFECT

Hold out both index fingers in front of you as though they were guns, about one foot apart; you can check this by having a friend put a ruler on your fingers. So now you are supporting a ruler with a finger at each end. The idea is slowly to move the fingers inwards towards each other. Curiously, the ruler can't fall off, it seems to adjust itself to prevent it; you will also find it impossible to prevent your fingers meeting at the exact centre of the ruler. How does this happen?

$\mathcal{S}$ECRET

The ruler is always in balance because friction increases as the weight of an end increases so, try as you may to have your fingers meet anywhere other than the middle of the ruler, it just won't happen. This is an effect that all your friends can try, maybe the whole class.

The Third Hand

This intriguing sequence of eerie effects demonstrates how a magician can fool an assistant in both sensory and physiological ways at the same time.

Effect

The magician runs the tips of both index fingers very softly down an assistant's face and repeats the gesture three or four times; then the assistant is asked to close his eyes. The magician keeps stroking his fingertips down from the assistant's forehead, across his eyes, on to his cheeks, back to his forehead, across his eyes, down his cheeks, repetitively, without a break in the rhythm. Suddenly the magician stops, the tips of both index fingers are resting lightly on the assistant's closed eyes. And yet the assistant feels that someone or something has tapped the back of his head twice. The magician runs his fingertips down to the assistant's cheeks and commands the assistant to open his eyes to witness the magician remove both fingertips from his cheeks. There is nobody else around who could have tapped the back of his head, so how could it happen? Is there a ghost in the house?

Secret

This trick is dependent on a combination of techniques: the rhythmic repetition of stroking the fingers down the assistant's face and, without any change of pace or break in the rhythm, the substitution of one finger for another.

To practise this, point both forefingers out as you bend the other fingers into the palms of each hand and cover them with your thumbs. Now place both fingertips on the table about $2\frac{1}{2}$ inches (6cms) apart and lightly stroke them down in unison, about

4 inches (10cms) across the surface of the table. Then take them off the table, put them back to your start point and do it again. Repeat this a few times, building up a set rhythm, getting the feel of this rhythm.

Then, when you reach the end of a downward stroke – and as you remove your fingertips from the table ready to replace them again at your start point – extend the middle finger of your right hand and put the fingertips of your right-hand forefinger and middle finger on the start point and gently stroke them down. Do this without breaking rhythm. Your left

forefinger is not placed at the start point on the table. So what you have done is to introduce your middle finger and substitute your right forefinger for your left forefinger, thereby leaving your left hand completely free to do the sneaky bit.

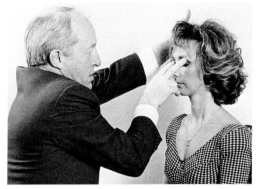

Continue practising by stroking the table with your right fingertips, then stop at the point you would judge to be the assistant's eyes, tap the table twice with the fingertips of your left hand, continuing stroking, and switch your left forefinger back to replace your right forefinger as you continue to stroke.

If you have read the above carefully you'll know it's a very simple sequence, but it needs practice to do it well. So, having mastered the art of amazing a tabletop, you will need to practise on a willing friend to become expert in the art of amazing real people. Remember, at the end of the trick as you remove your right fingertips from the assistant's closed eyes, quickly switch your left forefinger into position as you fold your right middle finger into the palm of your right hand. Do this as you instruct your assistant to open his eyes. He will have seen nothing, yet felt ... well, who knows what he thinks he has felt?

Control

Follow The Third Hand with this spooky item.

Effect

A spectator is instructed to clasp his hands together with fingers interlocked, then to extend both forefingers upright so his fingers and hands are pointing to the ceiling at eye level. The extended fingers must be held in this position with a gap of about $\frac{1}{4}$ of an inch ($\frac{1}{2}$ a centimetre) between them. The magician then explains that, sticking out of the fingernails of each extended finger, is a tiny, invisible wheel. And, as the magician turns these little wheels, the gap between the fingertips will close until they are touching.

Secret

The method is part psychology and part physiology. As you perform the trick tell the spectator to relax and watch the little invisible wheels as you turn them. Point out that the fingertips are slowly coming together. What you are really inducing him to do is to relax the muscles of the fingers. Holding the fingers upright with a gap between them creates tension in the muscles. At your suggestion the muscles are slowly relaxed and, involuntarily, the fingertips will meet.

And the little invisible wheels? Well, that's just a little hokum and bunkum that we magicians use to divert people's attention during the presentation of a trick.

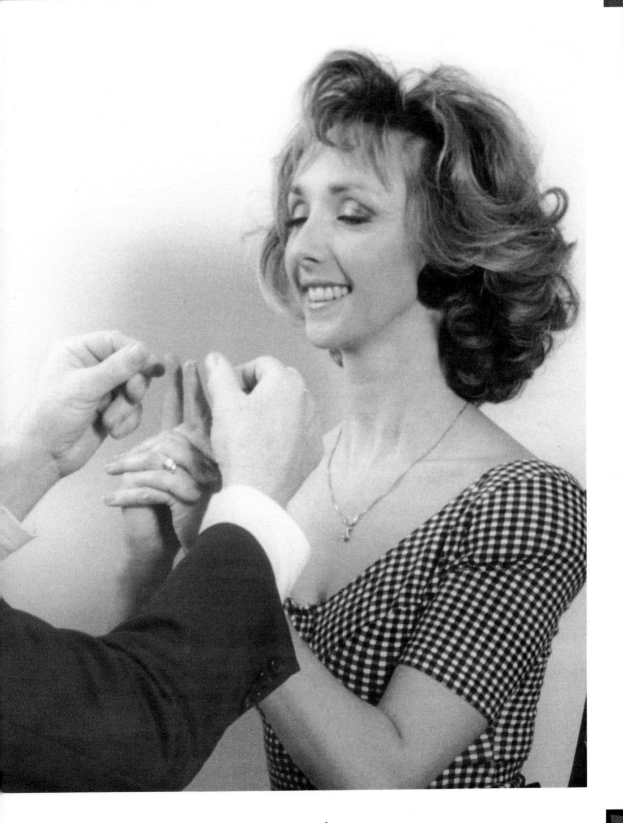

Conetradiction

Although not strictly a magic trick, this visual effect is very magical as it appears to defy the law of gravity.

Effect

The magician exhibits a strange-looking, double-cone type of object. This is not really so strange because it is actually made of two cones that have been glued together at their bottom edges. He has also arranged two stacks of books and two pencils in such a way as to create a sort of track or railway line which the magic cone will run along. All well and good so far, except that the pencils are not horizontal, they are angled so the magic cone will roll down them; curiously, the cone does not run down, it rolls up, all by itself, obviously paying not the slightest attention to gravity.

Secret

Make two cones out of stiff paper or thin card; use glue or rubber cement to stick them together, running a thin line of glue round the bottom edge of one cone and sticking it to the bottom edge of the other one. The end result will be your very own magic cone. Now make two stacks of books so that one stack is about half to a third the height of the other. Place the books about 5 to 6 inches (12–15cms) apart and then carefully place both pencils across to bridge the gap between the books – like a sloping railway line. Now, and here is the experimental bit, arrange the pencils so that the lower ends are about one inch (2½cms) apart and the top ends are wider apart, about the length of the cone itself should be about right.

Now place the double cone across the pencils at their lower ends and what should happen is that the magic cone will roll up the pencils. If that doesn't immediately happen you will have to experiment by varying the angle of the slope of the pencils and their distance apart. Just play with it awhile and you will get it, because it's actually the size of the cones that determines the angle and varying width of the pencils. So a little trial will ultimately produce no error.

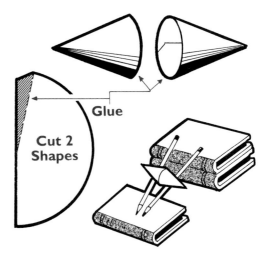

Cut 2 Shapes

Glue

And the real secret is that, although the cone may look as though it is contradicting the law of gravity, it is, in fact, proving that law. If you look at the cone from the side you will see that its centre of gravity really moves down as it moves 'up', as the increasing width of the railway-line pencils actually lowers the cone's centre of gravity. The magic of science!

Bendy Pencil

Everybody knows that pencils are straight and solid. Everybody except a magician, that is.

Effect

Holding a pencil near one end, horizontally to the floor, the great wonder worker shakes it up and down, creating the very real visual illusion of its bending as though it were made of soft rubber.

Secret

Hold the pencil near one end, between the thumb (underneath) and forefinger (on top) of your right hand or your left if you are left-handed. Now make a series of rapid, short, up-and-down shakes, at the same time slightly loosening your grip on the pencil so that it wobbles between the tips of your finger and thumb. Don't alter the tempo of the shaking movement, study the movement of the pencil and you will gradually see the visual effect of a soft, bendy pencil. You will need to play with it to get the exact tempo and feel that suits you. One tip is not to be too frantic, just nice, consistent up-and-down movements no greater than 2 or 3 inches (5–8cms) will do it. Try it in front of a mirror to best see the effect.

This, happily, is a fun type of trick you can share with your friends.

The Top-and-Bottom Trick

Here is a 'funnyosity' for you.

Effect

A piece of paper with the word Top on it is placed on top of a piece of paper with the word Bottom on it. Both pieces are folded around a pencil and then unrolled to reveal the word Bottom on top of the word Top.

Secret

Cut two pieces of paper about the size of a £20 note. Write the word Bottom in capitals, horizontally along the length of one piece, then put the second piece vertically on top of the Bottom piece, to make a capital letter T. Then write the word Top, in capitals, along the length of this piece.

So you now have two pieces of paper. Top is on top and Bottom is underneath (*see photo 1*). Make sure that the edges of both pieces furthest away from your body are in alignment. Now place a pencil, horizontally, on top of the edge nearest your body and carefully roll the pencil away from you (*see photo 2*), wrapping the papers around the pencil as you roll it. When you reach the top edge of the Top piece, stop (*see photo 3*). Then, just as carefully, roll the pencil back towards you, unwrapping the papers as you do so. This will result in the Bottom piece being on top and the Top piece being on the bottom (*see photo 4*). This proves that anything, or anyone, at the bottom can get to the top.

1

2

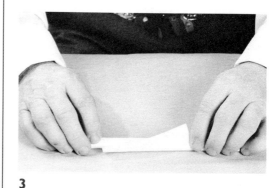

3

4

Magnetic

Here is a very nice sequence of visual tricks using your ruler.

*E*FFECT

The classroom magician demonstrates his magnetic control over a ruler which, in apparent defiance of the law of gravity, sticks to his hands in a variety of ways.

*S*ECRET

We are really combining several different methods in this sequence, each of them appearing to be progressively more impossible.

THREE VERSIONS

First effect The magician holds a ruler in his left hand and talks about personal magnetism. Offering to demonstrate his powers in this area he clasps his hands together with his fingers interlocked, the backs of his hands facing the spectators, the ends of the ruler held in a vertical position, sticking out above and below his hands. Nothing magical so far. The magician then opens his hands, so they are straight but with fingers still interlocked. The ruler looks as though it is sticking to the insides of his interlocked fingers. Well, it would do if both thumbs could be seen.

Pretending to hear somebody mention that, the magician responds by sticking his left thumb up, then he pretends to hear a murmur about his right thumb which is still hidden and obviously holding the ruler in place. The magician responds by sticking his right thumb up; this would be impressive if he hadn't, at the same time, lowered his left thumb behind his fingers to hold the ruler in place. Seeming to hear another grumble, he says innocently, 'The left thumb, no problem.' And promptly pops it into sight again; unfortunately, he just as promptly pops the right thumb out of sight. Apparently realising by now that the spectators are not overly impressed he says, 'Oh, you mean both thumbs.' And promptly pops both thumbs into view. Now there is nothing holding the ruler in place, as the magician demonstrates by rocking his arms gently from side to side. Still the ruler stays in place. He then says, 'Go,' and the ruler drops an inch (2cms) and stops as he says, 'Stop.' The magician does this a couple more times, then clasps his hands together and separates them as he offers the ruler for examination.

First secret If you were to study the magician's interlocked fingers closely from in front, and counted them, you would count (including thumbs) only nine, and that's the secret. It's quite possible to interlock your fingers in such a way that the right middle finger is free on the inside of your left hand and not, as is normal, on the outside. The ruler is held in between the base of the left fingers and the back of the right middle finger. You'll have to practise easing the grip sufficiently for the ruler to slide down in stages, but it's not difficult. The rest is presentation. Having shown this trick you progress to a variation.

Second effect Taking the ruler the magician rubs it vigorously on his left sleeve, 'to create static', and holds the ruler in the middle in his left hand. Gripping the inside of his left wrist with his right hand he turns side on with his left shoulder facing the spectators and suddenly opens his left hand with fingers wide apart. And again the ruler appears to stick, this time to the palm of his left hand. Closing his left hand, he takes the ruler with his right hand and rubs it

against his sleeve again, 'to regenerate the
static electricity'. And repeats the effect.
The trick is finished by handing the ruler
out again for examination.

Second secret When you grip the inside
of your left wrist with your right hand, you
will find that it's possible to stick your right
index finger into your left palm, and that is
how you hold the ruler in place.

There may be some people who are
familiar with this method. If there are, you
knock them out with the next variation.

Third effect The magician performs what,
at first sight, appears to be the second
effect all over again. There is one difference.
If somebody should challenge him to take
his right hand away from his left wrist, he
does so. The ruler really does seem to stick
to his left hand.

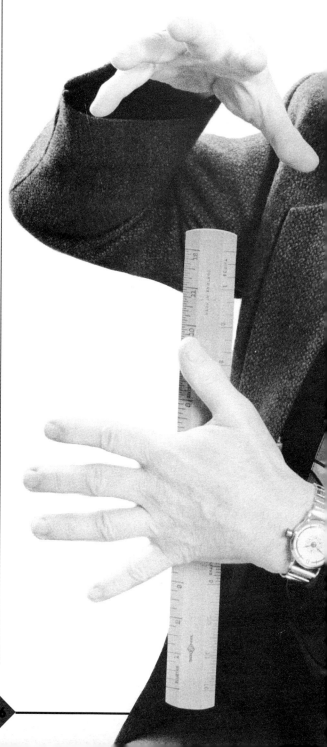

Third secret If you wear a watch on your left wrist you are, for all practical purposes, ready to learn this version. The only other item you will need is, preferably, a pocket comb, but a pencil will do. Put the comb under the wristband of your watch so that one end projects into the palm of your left hand. Put the ruler between the comb and your palm and you'll quickly get sufficient feel as to how much pressure will be needed to hold the ruler in place. At the end of the trick, when you hand the ruler out for examination, just push the comb out of sight up your sleeve.

Performed with pace, not overly quickly, but definitely not slowly, it's a very nice sequence.

a Bit Missing

Magicians are funny people, they will fiddle about with anything if there is magic in it. Even the laws of mathematics are not sacred. Here is a very interesting bit of magic that you can have fun with in your maths class at school.

*E*FFECT

A measured square of cardboard, when assembled one way as a four-piece rectangle, is 65 inches square (415 square centimetres). When assembled another way, it is 64 inches square (413 square centimetres). One square inch has vanished. Or has it just gone missing?

*S*ECRET

From a piece of thin cardboard cut out an 8 inch by 8 inch (23cm × 23cm) square. Then, using your ruler, measure and draw three straight lines on the card, exactly as illustrated. Boldly ink in the letters A, B, C, D exactly as shown, and then carefully cut along the lines with a pair of scissors. This will give you four separate pieces of card, lettered A, B, C and D.

To present the effect assemble the pieces of card in a rectangular shape, as shown. Now ask a friend to measure the long bottom edge and then the short side, and multiply them together to get the total number of square inches. So the sum will be 13 inches × 5 inches = 65 square inches. Now reassemble the pieces in the shape of a square. Then ask the same friend to

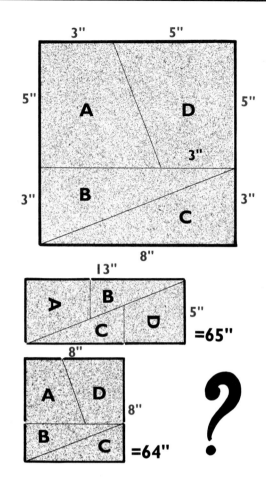

measure and multiply the top edge and the side edge to get the total number of square inches. The sum will be 8 inches × 8 inches = 64 square inches.

So what happened to the missing inch? You may like to ask your maths teacher to help you diddle the riddle. I'll give you one clue. When the pieces are in the rectangular shape, is it a genuine rectangle? Only two of the corners are right angles and, whilst the other two appear to be, they cannot be proven to be. That's not really as confusing as it seems, it's actually the real secret of the missing inch. It just goes to show that there really is such a thing as 'mathemagic'!!

Twenty Tricks from Your Pockets

Whilst not necessarily major magic, the following stunts have mysterious aspects that will puzzle spectators. They are also fun to do and use everyday objects found in most households – you can easily carry these in your pockets.

Coin Vanish Number One

Effect

The magician spins a small coin, a 1p or £1 will do fine, on a hard-topped surface. As it is spinning he slaps a matchbox straight down on top of it and instantly lifts the matchbox up. The spinning coin has vanished.

Secret

Remove most, or all, of the matches from a wooden (not cardboard) matchbox. Hold the box horizontally by the long edges and practise smacking the bottom of the box down on a hard table surface and, the split second it hits the surface, lifting it straight

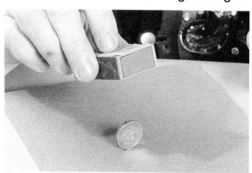

back up. One thing to bear in mind when practising is that the matchbox should go straight down and straight up, in a more or less vertical line – not an arc. The danger with striking the coin in an arc is that the coin may squirt out from under the matchbox if it hits it at an angle because, as you've probably gathered by now, the impact of the matchbox causes the coin to penetrate the brittle bottom of the box.

The fact that the coin is spinning makes the all-important difference: the matchbox is guaranteed to hit the top edge of the coin, thus forcing it through the base of the matchbox.

Practise for speed. It's the instant smack down and straight up that creates the effect. One moment the coin is there, a split second later it isn't. Don't show anyone the bottom of the matchbox, just put it away in your pocket. It is more magical to present this as a curiosity, 'Have you ever seen this?' Present it briskly, and leave them wondering. Just in case Mum objects to your doing this on her nice wooden table top, use a tray and make her happy.

Coin Vanish Number Two

If you can snap your fingers you are capable of performing a very startling vanish of a small coin. A 5p is perfect.

Effect

Holding the coin between the pads of his thumb and middle finger, his hand in the shape he would make if he were going to 'snap his fingers', the magician does just that and the coin instantly vanishes.

Secret

Two of the oldest clichés people use when talking about magicians are: 'It's all done by mirrors,' and 'It's up his sleeve.' In this case the latter is absolutely true, the coin does go up your sleeve. You will need to roll up your right shirt-sleeve and put on a jacket.

Hold your arm out, slightly to the right, horizontally to the floor. The back of your hand faces upwards, towards the ceiling. The effect of this will be that the cuff of your right sleeve will be hanging down, creating an opening between its lower edge and the underside of your wrist. It's into this tunnel the coin will go at such a speed that the human eye can't follow it. As a guide to practising this, hold the coin in the position described and also hold your arm out, creating the tunnel. You will see that it is the middle finger that propels the coin up the sleeve when you snap your fingers. That's the secret of it. So, if you find that the coin misses the sleeve, or hits the cuff, just adjust your hand position; also, raising the right elbow so it's slightly higher than the wrist will help.

To present the effect, hold the coin up in front of your body, say, 'Now you see it,' as you turn your hand over and raise your arm into position, then say, 'Now you don't,' as you snap vanish it. Keep your arm up and open your fingers wide and, with a flourish, turn your hand over to show that it is empty. Obviously, if you do this trick standing up, you won't lower your arm completely in case the coin falls out; you only do that when nobody is looking so the coin will drop into your cupped fingers.

Performed snappily (pun intended) it's an excellent vanish. If anybody should dare to suggest, 'It's up your sleeve,' you may care to respond with something along the lines of, 'You don't believe that old cliché, do you? Mind you, I do keep a rabbit up there, so who knows?'

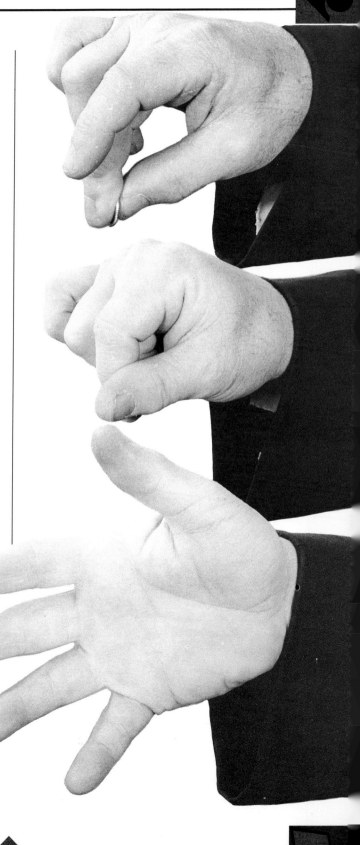

Tricky Tunnel

This is another nice pocket item with a new, additional finish.

Effect

Knots vanish, and become separated, in the most extraordinary way.

Two versions

First effect The magician ties a piece of string around the outer cover of a matchbox (minus the inner box) (*see photo 1*). Then he feeds one end of the string through the cover (*see photos 2 and 3*) and carefully eases the knot off the outside of the cover and into the tunnel (*see photo 4*), so it's hidden from view. A spectator is given both ends of the string to hold. The magician makes a practised magic wave over the box, utters his favourite magic word, and slides the cover along to the end of the string (*see photo 5*) to show that the knot has disappeared.

Second effect This takes us up to the point where the knot is inside the cover and the ends of the string are held by the spectator. Instead of the knot vanishing the magician tips the cover up and the knot falls out of it, having apparently leapt off the string. This is confirmed by examining the string and the cover.

Secret

Each of the two versions has its own trick.

First secret The first version is performed exactly as described and it will finish exactly as described. It works itself. By putting one end of the string through the cover and then the knot – pulling the string acts to untie itself. The pretence is in the knot being in the cover, it isn't; it doesn't exist.

Second secret This is stronger. All you do is prepare a small knot made from the same string, that you carry in your pocket.

To make the knot appear, hold it loosely in the cupped fingers of your left hand and, when the knot is (supposedly) in the tunnel, hold the cover by its long edges with your right hand, which goes underneath the cover, right thumb on the long side nearest to you and fingertips on the long side nearest the spectator who is holding the string. Pull the cover a little towards you and, in one motion, raise your left hand to meet the cover which the right hand is tipping upright anticlockwise. Coincide it so the left, open end of the cover is put straight on to your left fingers and over the knot as the hands meet. It should appear that you have placed the cover in an upright position on your left hand for support to enable you to look down inside the cover.

At this moment you notice the knot inside the cover which you lift from your fingers better to show it to your spectator. A comment, along the lines of, 'Wow, look at that! It came right off the string,' should strike the right note.

For the move to be convincing, your attention should be on the matchbox cover and the little bit of magic inside it; pay no attention to the left hand at all, even when you reveal the knot – which is what everyone will look at. Don't worry about holding the knot in your curled fingers, nobody knows it's there so you don't need to feel guilty about it.

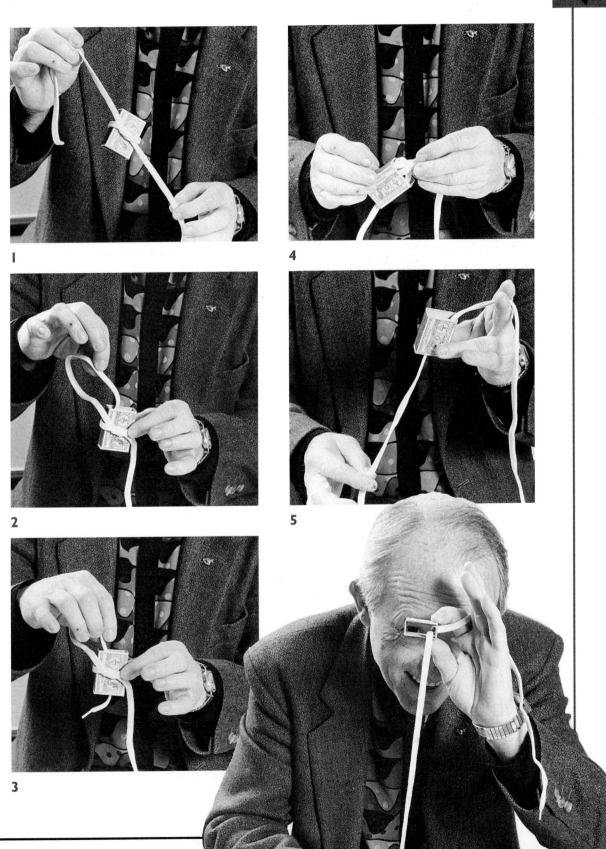

1

2

3

4

5

Penny Puzzles

The world of magic and the world of puzzles find common ground in those interesting and amusing effects and stunts that are generally labelled 'Betchas'. Always fun to try, here is a magician's potpourri that you can present any time, anywhere.

Effect

Place three pennies on any flat smooth surface so that the edges of penny one and penny two are touching and penny number three is in line with the other two, but about $1\frac{1}{2}$ inches (4cms) away from penny number two.

Issue the following challenge to your friends: 'I betcha can't move penny number three to a position between pennies one and two without moving penny number two from its position and without touching penny number one in any way at all.'

Secret

To do the trick, press your left fingertip on to penny number two and, with your right

middle finger, push penny number three sharply towards the edge of penny number two, releasing your finger at the last second as the coin forcibly hits the edge of penny number two. The force of the strike will knock penny number one away from number two, allowing you to put penny three between pennies one and two.

Easy Peasy

Sometimes the simplest of puzzles baffles the brightest of people. This puzzle is easy, but how easy is easy? Try it and find out for yourself.

Effect

Six coins are laid out in a row (with edges touching) in the following order. From left to right coins one, two and three are heads up and coins four, five and six are tails up.

The puzzle is to arrange them in head, tail, head, tail, head, tail order in three moves. At each move you must turn over two touching coins at a time. For example, coins one and two together, or coins five and six, or four and five, whatever you decide, but only three moves are allowed.

SECRET

Like all such secrets, it's easy when you know how. In this case the puzzle is solved by the following sequence. Turn over coins

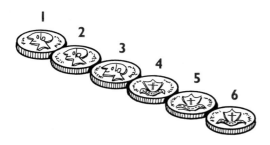

three and four, four and five and two and three. Easy peasy; now try it on your friends.

But How?

Here is an amusing swindle that's perfect for the lunch table.

EFFECT

A penny is placed on a table that is covered with a smooth linen or cotton tablecloth. Two 10p pieces are placed either side of the penny to support a tumbler which is placed, mouth down, over the penny (*see photo 1*). This makes a very low bridge under which the penny can be removed. The problem is to remove the penny without touching the glass, the supporting coins or using any implement to poke or pull the penny from under the tumbler. In fact, you are not even allowed to touch the penny. It is possible, but how?

SECRET

Pull the tablecloth taut away from you with your left hand in line with the penny, then with the fingernail of your right index finger vigorously scratch the tablecloth just in front of the rim of the tumbler nearest to you, in line with the penny and the taut cloth (*see photo 2*). The penny will move, by itself, all the way out from under the glass (*see photo 3*). That's how!

1

2

3

Two for One

Here a neat swindle and a magic puzzle are combined to good effect.

Effect

The magician shows a piece of paper that is 5 inches (13cms) square. In the centre of the paper is a small hole which he shows to be exactly the size of a 1p coin. Offering the paper and a 10p piece to a spectator he asks if it is possible to push the coin through the small hole without it tearing the paper. Assuming the answer is negative, the magician demonstrates not one, but two, ways of doing just that.

Secret

The first solution is really a gag. Put the 10p coin on the table, hold the paper in your left hand, take a pencil in your right hand, put it halfway through the hole in the paper and *push* the coin on the table with the end of the pencil.

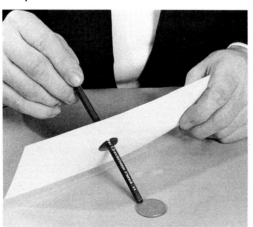

The second solution is to fold the paper in half; don't crease it, just create a valley into which you place the 10p coin so it sits in the open fold of the hole. Now, holding

the folded paper between thumbs and fingers, on either side of the hole, slowly bend the ends of the paper upwards and towards each other. This has the effect of considerably widening the width of the hole, sufficiently for the coin to drop completely through it. Unfold the paper,

straighten out any creases and you have performed a very neat trick. For those not in the know it is a nice item.

To prepare the paper put a 1p coin on the centre of the paper and very carefully draw round its circumference with a pencil until you have completed a circle. Then, just as carefully, cutting fractionally inside the pencil line, cut this circle out of the paper with your scissors.

3 Pence

You shouldn't believe your eyes in this trick, but you can't help believing what you can clearly see! Or can you?

Effect

The Great Magical Marvel (that's you) rubs two 1p coins together, quickly, in short, up-and-down movements. And strangely, for all to see, a third penny appears between the other two. The GMM (that's still you) drops all three coins on to the table and the mysterious third coin instantly vanishes, leaving the two original pennies.

Secret

This trick is really an optical illusion. Hold two pennies together between the tips of your index fingers pointing up at about eye level. Then with short, quick, up-and-down movements rub the pennies together. This will create the optical effect of a third penny appearing between, and slightly below, the other two coins.

What actually happens is that the retinas of your eyes retain the image of the two coins at their lowest point, as they are vigorously rubbed together. Keep rubbing the coins together as you lower your hands, then instantly move your fingers apart and the third penny will vanish as the other two drop on to the table.

Practise this and you will have added a super, little, do-it-anywhere, any time trick to your repertoire.

The Lazy Magician

Before you show this clever effect to anyone try it on yourself and I guarantee you will be fooled. This is one of those rare tricks in which, when performing it for others, you don't even have to touch the cards. You simply direct operations; it is perfect for a lazy magician. Try it with the cards in your hands as you read the Effects and you will see how easy it is to do.

Effect

Under the direction of the magician a spectator spells out and finds his own mentally selected card.

Secret

The secret is to follow the instructions, then the cards will automatically fall into the right position.

Two Versions

First effect I will describe this as though you were doing it for yourself. Deal three piles of seven cards, face down, on the table. Put the rest of the pack aside. Pick up any pile, look at the faces of the cards, and mentally select and remember any one of the cards. Turn the cards in your hands face down and put them on top of one of the piles on the table. Pick up the remaining pile of seven cards and put it on top of the others, making one pile.

Pick up the cards and deal them into three new piles by dealing one card down for the first, the second card for the second pile, the third card for the third, then back to the beginning, the fourth card on the first pile, fifth on the second, sixth on the third, seventh on the first pile, and so on in rotation until all the cards are dealt.

Now have a guess which pile you think your card is in. Pick up the pile and take a look. If you see your card turn the cards face down and put them on top of one of the other piles and, just as before, put the remaining pile on top of the others, making one pile. If your card is not in the pile of your choice place the cards face down in a pile in the position they were in. Pick up another pile and look for your card again. If you see it put the cards face down on top of one of the other piles, and place the remaining pile on top. If you don't see your card, put them back on the table in their original position. Your card will obviously now be in the last pile of cards; pick them up, look at the faces, check your card is there and put them face down on one of the piles on the table and put the last pile on top of those.

Now deal out three new piles in the same way as before, dealing one, two, three cards as the start of each pile, then continue dealing in rotation. Have another guess which pile your card may be in and take a look as you did before, except this time, when you find the pile with your card in, turn it face down, keep it in your hands and do the following deal. You are going to move one card for each letter as you spell out the following sentence:

THAT! IS! THE! CARD! YOU! TOOK!

Take the top card from the pile in your hands and put it underneath the pile so it now becomes the bottom card. Do this as

you spell out aloud the letter T. Take the next card for the letter H and put it underneath, the next for the letter A, the next for the letter T, and the next card deal face down on to the table for the exclamation mark.

Deal another card from top to bottom, of the cards you are holding, for the letter I, another top to bottom for S, then deal the next card on to the table for the exclamation mark.

Start again. Top to bottom for T, again for H, again for E. Then the next card on to the table for the exclamation mark.

Again in the hands, top to bottom for C, also for A, the same for R and again for D. Then deal the next card on to the table for the exclamation mark. (Remember the cards are face down all the time you are doing this.)

Start again for Y, top to bottom. Top to bottom for O, again for U; then the next card on to the table.

You will now have only two cards left. Transfer each in turn from top to bottom as you spell TOOK then deal the top card on to the table. You will be holding one card face down in your hands and I want you to imagine my voice whispering the following sentence in your ear as you turn the card face up.

'That is the card you took.' And it will be!

First secret If you do the trick as described you can't fail. I'll summarise the sequence to make it easy for you to practise.

1 Deal three piles, in rotation, seven cards in each pile.

2 Select a card from one pile, then make sure that that pile is sandwiched between the other two.

3 Deal three more piles, in rotation, seven cards in each pile.

4 Find the pile that has the selected card in it and make sure it is again the middle pile when the cards are gathered up, sandwiched between the other two.

5 Deal three more piles in rotation, seven cards in each pile.

6 Find the pile with the selected card in it and perform the spelling and discard procedure; this will always end with the revelation of the chosen card.

Second effect If you are asked to perform the trick again for the same audience, the following variation will come in handy. This version uses three piles of nine cards each, so twenty-seven cards are used instead of

twenty-one. Perform the Effect exactly as before except that, when you come to the spelling at the end, you use the following sentence. Moving one card from top to bottom for each letter you spell, and dealing one card on to the table for each capital letter at the end of each word, note that the third word A is dealt on to the table:

y o U t o o K A c a r D a n D t h i S i S i T

To present these tricks as a lazy magician you must exercise complete control of the spectators' actions because, if the chosen card doesn't remain in the position it was in when selected, the tricks won't work. The same rule applies to the order of the piles; the chosen card pile must go in the middle of the other two every time.

If you can ensure that the spectators do not touch the cards, the tricks are safer to do. You can then concentrate on the presentation in which you challenge them to see how good they are at guessing the pile with 'their' card in, or you can present the tricks as a guide as to whether or not they are lucky at cards.

These tricks may seem to be lengthy but the effect isn't so in performance. One final tip that will help you to practise the tricks is that, once you have chosen a card, turn this selected card face up in its pile, then proceed through the gathering, dealing and, finally, spelling parts of the tricks. I suggest this because most tricks of this type go wrong because the procedure isn't strictly followed. It only needs one card to be misdealt or mis-spelt and the tricks will fail. Turning a chosen card face up for practice purposes should also give you a big clue to the mathematical formula that makes the tricks work.

Tip-up

Origami, the ancient Japanese art of paper folding, is regarded by magicians as an allied art. It is related to magic because it's fun and full of wonders.

Here is an amusing paper fold that is fun for a number of people to try together. We had an audience full of spectators who tried doing it in one of our programmes; the result was a riot. Try it for yourself.

EFFECT

The magician folds a small square of paper into a triangular shape and carefully places it on the table. Then, as if by magic, the folded paper slowly tips itself upright in a most eerie fashion.

SECRET

It's all in the folding. To fold the tip-up you will need a square of paper that creases well when folded, so the paper should be

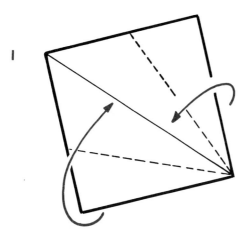

1

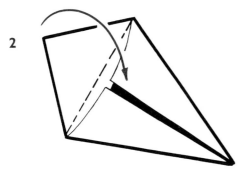

2

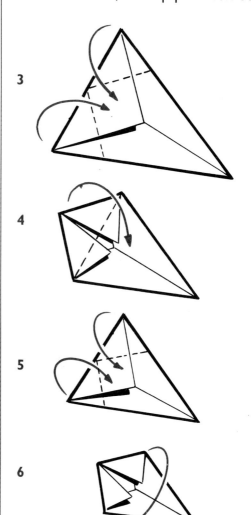

3

4

5

6

crisp and not too soft. Make each crease by using your thumbnail or a ruler. When you have completed your folding (by following the diagrams) put the tip-up on the table on its longer open side. The tip-up will slowly (very slowly) stand up on its shorter edges. The idea is to get it to tip up as slowly as possible. You might like to time it with your watch. A piece of paper 4 inches × 4 inches (10cms × 10cms) is about the right size to use. You can also purchase pre-cut Origami paper from art supply shops.

$\mathcal{I}$nto $\mathcal{T}$hin $\mathcal{A}$ir

This is the way to vanish any small object, like a coin or a ring, in a handkerchief.

$\mathcal{E}$FFECT

The small object is dropped into the handkerchief. The magician utters his favourite magic word – A B R A C A D A B R A! The handkerchief is thrown high into the air as the magician claps his hands. The small object doesn't fall, it has vanished. Catching the handkerchief the magician holds it by one corner and shakes it. The object has definitely vanished. Then, holding the handkerchief bunched in his left hand, the magician shows his right hand empty, reaches into the handkerchief and takes out the missing object!

$\mathcal{S}$ECRET

For this neat trick you will need a handkerchief, the loan of any small object – coin, ring, button, etc. – and a small rubber band.

Secretly place the rubber band over the thumb, index finger and middle fingers of your left hand. Then shake the handkerchief with your right hand and drape it over your left hand. Ask a friend to drop the small object into the handkerchief. Now, ease the rubber band off your fingers and over the small object so that it encloses the object like a pocket. You will now be able to throw the handkerchief into the air without the object falling out. You will also be able to hold the handkerchief by one corner and gently shake it, the object being held securely in place in its secret pocket by the elastic band. To retrieve the borrowed object just reach into the crumpled handkerchief, showing your hand empty first, and take out the object from the pocket. Then put the handkerchief away.

Practise this a few times and you will get the hang of it. Performed briskly, this is a mysterious little trick.

Gypsy Fortune Teller

Here is a paper fold that will give you a lot of fun. Your friends will enjoy this. Here's what to do.

1 Take a square of paper about 7 inches (18cms) each side.

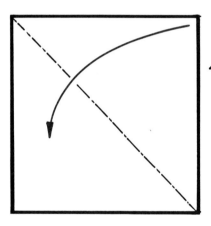

2 Fold in half diagonally.

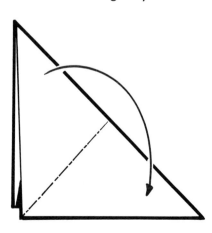

3 Fold in half again.

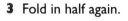
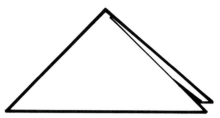

4 Open it up, turn it over and fold each of the four corners into the centre.

5 Turn it over and fold the corners into the centre.

TURN OVER

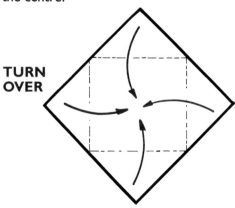

6 Now open it up and write the words and numbers on the paper as illustrated.

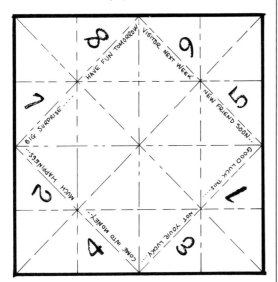

7 Turn it over and fold the corners into the centre, so you will be seeing only the numbers. Don't open it up.

8 Turn it over, so the words are face up, and fold the four corners into the centre. The numbers will appear again.

9 Now fold the packet in half and you will see that there are four flaps. Slide your left thumb and first finger under the left top and bottom flaps and your right thumb and first finger under the right top and bottom flaps.

10 Now pinch the packet between thumbs and fingertips, push in and you will form a rough pyramid shape.

11 Now, by opening and closing the fingers and thumbs in one direction you will see numbers 1 to 4 and, in the other direction, numbers 5 to 8.

To present this, open the fortune teller and ask a friend to choose a number between 1 and 4. If he chooses, for example, number 4, open and close the fortune teller each way four times. Then ask him to choose another number that he can see, then open and close that number of times. Finally, ask him to choose another number that he can see, now open and fold back that flap to reveal his fortune. Here is what you say for each fortune:

1 'You will have good luck this week.'
2 'You will have much happiness tomorrow.'
3 'This is not your lucky day.'
4 'You will come into some money soon.'
5 'You will soon meet a new friend.'
6 'You will get a visitor to your home next week.'
7 'You are in for a big surprise next month.'
8 'You will have fun with your friends tomorrow.'

Remember to make each folded crease nice and sharp by pressing it with a ruler or pencil. Coloured paper always looks better than plain white. You don't have to stick to the fortunes I have listed here. Try making up your own; the more mysterious they are the more your friends will enjoy them. Good examples can be found in the star signs and astrology columns of newspapers and magazines.

Elastic Jumpers

This trick shows how to make two elastic bands change places on your fingers by magic.

EFFECT

The magician puts a red elastic band over the first and second fingers of his left hand and over his third and fourth fingers he puts a green elastic band. He bends his fingers into his fist and, when he opens his hand again, the elastic bands have changed places.

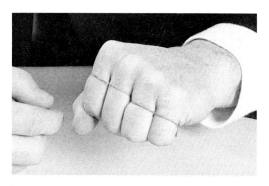

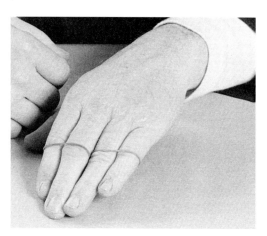

SECRET

Hold your left hand flat; now open your fingers, keeping your first and second and third and fourth fingers together so there is a gap between your second and third fingers.

1 We'll refer to your first and second fingers as A and your third and fourth fingers as B.

2 Put the red band over A, letting it slide to the base of the fingers.

3 Put the green band over B in the same way.

4 With your left palm facing you, hook your right index finger inside and stretch green band B across and over red band A. Your right index finger, which is inside band B, hooks inside band A.

5 Your right index finger stretches both bands downwards.

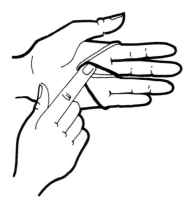

6 Put your right second finger in between the two bands alongside your index finger. Now open as wide a gap between your right index and second fingers as you can by spreading them sideways. This will create a triangle within the bands.

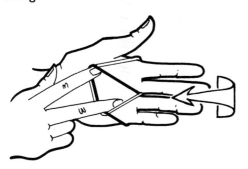

7 Fold all four fingers of your left hand down and into the triangle and take your right hand away, keeping your left fist closed. Both bands will now be over all four fingers of your left hand.

8 Now quickly straighten your left hand and open your fingers so there is a gap between your second and third fingers. The elastic bands will appear to jump across and instantly change places.

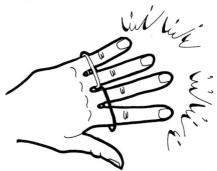

Bear in mind that the back of your left hand is the view that the spectator sees. Your left-hand palm is the side that faces you. As with all tricks smooth handling is the key to good performance. And smooth, confident handling can only be achieved with practice.

How to Put Your Head Completely through a Playing Card

This must read as the most ridiculous title imaginable except, my little magical believers, it is entirely possible as you will see.

Effect

Taking a single playing card from his pocket the magician asks his audience if they think it's possible for him, or anybody else, to put his head through a playing card. Some people may wonder why anyone in his right mind would want to put his head through a playing card. They are disbelievers. Most people just think it's impossible. This is where your friendly, local, neighbourhood magician (that should be you) comes in.

'Here is one I prepared earlier,' he says, fishing a playing card out of his pocket, that has been cut with great precision many times. The card is still flat but, as the magician gradually teases it open, it begins to stretch further and further apart until, finally, the magician can put his head right through it.

Secret

In this book we have taken great pains to give you descriptions of every effect and secret, even though there are numerous photographs and diagrams to help make understanding easy. But the preparation of this particular effect would take practically a whole chapter to describe without pictures. So we've used pictures only. As the old saying goes, one picture is worth a thousand words!

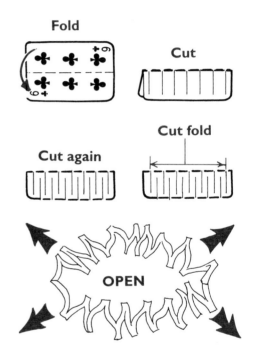

A couple of points to bear in mind: do watch your fingers when preparing the card and, secondly, note that the closer the cuts are to each other the larger the hole can be stretched. But it must be opened slowly and carefully so you don't tear it.

Some magicians say the hole can be made big enough for you to walk through. And you wouldn't disbelieve them, would you?

The Robbers, the Sheep and the Policeman

Of its type this is a classic little trick, easy to do and easy to learn. Performed at a good pace this little bit of mathemagic will puzzle your spectators. Inevitably, practice will polish your presentation.

Effect

Using seven 20p coins, the magician demonstrates the cautionary tale of two robbers who, hidden in two barns, attempt to steal five sheep from a field. All does not go well for the robbers, however, who resort to a safety plan to ensure they are not caught by the village constable. The trick illustrates the story, entertaining and baffling the spectators as it unfolds.

This is one of those strange tricks that is best understood by actually doing it, as it's almost impossible to explain the effect without doing it at the same time.

Secret

Five of the coins represent sheep. Lay them out, grouped together on the table. Place another coin to the left of the sheep; this we'll call Robber A. Place the last coin to the right of the sheep; this is Robber B.

SHEEP

Your left hand will represent a barn to the left, and your right hand a barn to the right. The barns are important because this is where the robbers intend to hide the sheep they steal.

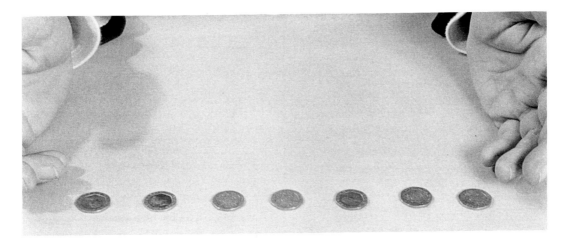

1 Robber A hides in the barn to the left. (Pick up the coin to the left and hold it in your closed left hand.)

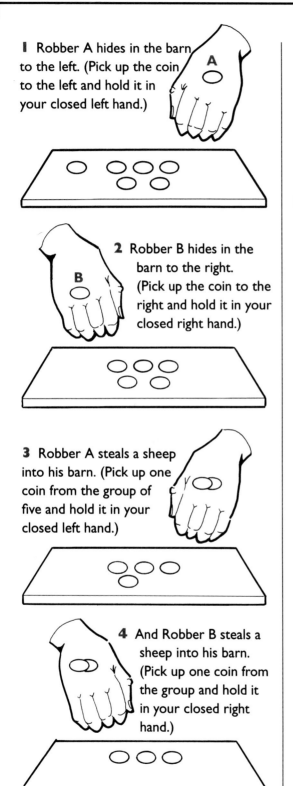

2 Robber B hides in the barn to the right. (Pick up the coin to the right and hold it in your closed right hand.)

3 Robber A steals a sheep into his barn. (Pick up one coin from the group of five and hold it in your closed left hand.)

4 And Robber B steals a sheep into his barn. (Pick up one coin from the group and hold it in your closed right hand.)

5 Robber A steals another sheep. (Pick up another coin and hold it in your closed left hand.)

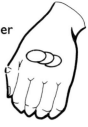

6 Robber B steals another sheep. (Pick up another coin and hold it in your closed right hand.)

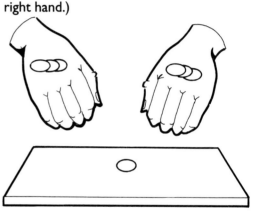

7 The last sheep is stolen by Robber A. (Pick up the last coin and hold it in your closed left hand.)

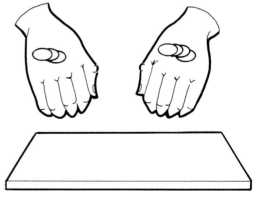

Suddenly, they hear the wailing siren of a police car! The robbers decide to get rid of the sheep as quickly as they can before the policeman arrives.

8 Robber B chases one sheep from his barn. (Put one coin back on to the middle of the table from your right hand.)

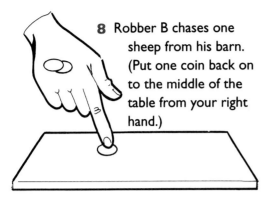

9 Robber A chases one sheep from his barn. (Put one coin back on to the middle of the table from your left hand.)

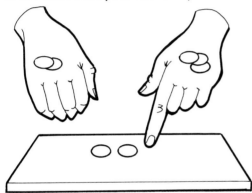

10 Robber B chases out a second sheep from his barn. (Put one more coin on to the middle of the table from your right hand.)

11 Robber A chases out another sheep. (Put another coin on to the table from your left hand.)

12 Robber B gets rid of his last sheep. (Put the last coin from your right hand on to the table.)

Suddenly, the robbers realise that the police-car siren is fading away into the distance. The policeman was chasing somebody else, not them. So, being robbers, they decide to steal the sheep all over again.

13 Robber A takes one sheep into his barn. (Pick up one coin from the table with your left hand.)

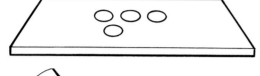

14 Robber B takes another sheep into his barn. (Pick up one coin from the table with your right hand.)

15 Another sheep for robber A. (Pick up one coin with your left hand.)

16 And another sheep for Robber B. (Pick up one coin with your right hand.)

17 And the last sheep is snaffled by Robber A. (Pick up the last coin with your left hand.)

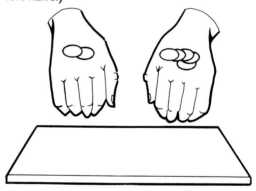

Suddenly there is the shrill sound of a policeman's whistle, followed shortly by the policeman arriving at the scene of the crime. He is followed, in turn, by the farmer who is carrying a shotgun! Not seeing any sheep they decide to search the barns. In the barn on the left they find five sheep happily munching hay. In the barn on the right they find the two robbers, pretending to be fast asleep. Since no sheep had been stolen from the farmer's property, the robbers had no case to answer for and, when woken up, were allowed to stroll away, free as birds. They were none the richer for their efforts, but, just possibly, a little wiser.

Tilt

Here is a nice quickie for the dinner table.

Effect

Taking a tumbler, half full of orange juice or milk, the magician positions it on the table in such a way that it appears to balance, tilted, on the rim of its base. The angle is not very great, but enough to puzzle.

Secret

In secret, or without anyone being aware of it, put a small piece of matchstick under the tablecloth about 6 to 8 inches (15–20cms) in from the edge of the table where you are sitting. It's this little piece of matchstick, about $\frac{1}{3}$ inch (1cm) long, on which you balance the bottom of the glass. Experiment with it and you'll find out how much of an angle it's possible to achieve. Have fun.

Have You Got What It Takes to be a Magician?

Presented as a qualification test to become a magician this neat trick will puzzle your friends because you can do it and they can't.

Effect

The magician carefully floats three matchsticks, in the shape of a triangle, in a bowl of water. They are arranged so that the ends of the matchsticks are not quite touching each other (*see photo 1*). He then invites his friends, one at a time, carefully and slowly to dip the ends of their index fingers into the water in the centre of the matchstick triangle. The object is to see if anything happens. Absolutely nothing happens until the last person, the magician, tries it. Then, mysteriously, the matchstick triangle gently floats apart and the matches drift to the edges of the bowl.

Secret

The magician has secretly rubbed a little soap on the end of his index fingertip (*see photo 2*). The soap reacts with the water to repel the matches (*see photo 3*). Secrets may be simple but the effects they create are everything!

1

2

3

$\mathcal{A}$ Matchstick, a Coin, a Bottle, and...?

Not only is this the title of this magical puzzle, they are the items you need to perform it.

$\mathcal{E}$ FFECT

A wooden matchstick is partially broken halfway along its length, sufficient to form the shape of a letter V. This is placed over the mouth of an empty bottle (*see photo 1*). On top of the V-shaped matchstick is placed a 5p coin so that it is over the mouth of the bottle (*see photo 2*). The problem you pose for a friend is how to get the coin into the bottle without touching the bottle, the coin or the matchstick. He can't bang the table or try to blow in the coin. The chances are that he will fail to solve it.

$\mathcal{S}$ ECRET

Provided the matchstick is only half broken, all you need to do is dip your little finger into some water (*see photo 3*) and let two or three drops drip on to the matchstick at the point where it is half broken (*see photo 4*). Now you can fill in the missing word in the title of the trick. That's all I'll tell you. Try it and see what happens for yourself. Then see if you can figure out why it happens.

1

2

3

4

A Test of Nerve

This trick is not for the faint hearted; you'll have to pluck up your courage the first time you try it. So be warned, it's not for those of a nervous disposition.

EFFECT

Exhibiting two clean, dry milk bottles and one crisp new banknote, that is also clean and dry, the magician stands one bottle upright and balances the other bottle upside down on top of it, so both bottles are mouth to mouth. But that's not all. In between the mouths of the bottles he has placed the banknote. The trick is to remove the banknote without touching or moving the bottles in any way at all.

SECRET

It's amazing how this trick worries people. It's probably because they can visualise the bottles falling over and breaking, and it does look so impossible.

But not to the magician. He boldly holds one end of the banknote taut in his left hand so it's horizontal (see *photo 1*) and, with his right index finger, sharply strikes down against the banknote about halfway between his left hand and the mouths of the bottles (see *photo 2*). The result? Exactly what you would expect of a magician. The banknote is free and the bottles are still balanced (see *photo 3*).

Although more a demonstration of skill and problem solving than great magic, this trick is worth practising because very few people will have ever seen it done.

1

2

3

The Puzzle Envelope

You might present this taxing little puzzle as a contest between your friends to see who can finish it quickest, assuming they can finish it at all!

EFFECT

The magician exhibits a drawing of the back of an envelope. The challenge to your friends is for them to study it for ten seconds, then to draw it in one continuous line, without taking their pencil off the paper or going over a line they've already drawn.

SECRET

The diagram should make everything clear. The corners of the envelope are numbered one to five; all you have to remember, in order to draw the envelope, is the following sequence of numbers: 1 to 2 to 3 to 4 to 5 to 3 to 1 to 4 to 2. Remember, you are drawing a continuous line to the corners of the envelope; do it a couple of times and it will stay in your memory forever. It's easy when you know how, it is not when you don't. If you find that one of your friends either knows this effect already, or has simply worked it out incredibly quickly, you can ask him to do it again. Only, this time, he must face a mirror and look into it as he draws on the paper. I can guarantee that this will slow him down considerably.

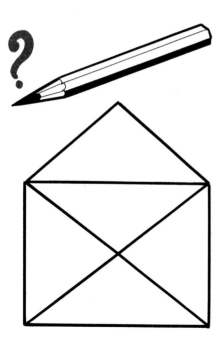

The Puzzle

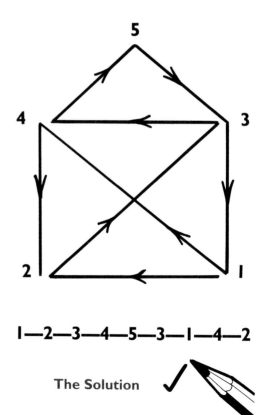

1—2—3—4—5—3—1—4—2

The Solution

Magic as Mentalism

As a new magician one of the most powerful branches of the conjurer's art that you must master is mentalism. Nothing is more mysterious than the ability to read minds and predict the course of future events. This chapter of strange secrets will add a dash of mysterioso to your repertoire, and the methods of mentalism will help you to appreciate that sometimes the secrets of magic are just as intriguing as the effects themselves.

Psychic Pencil

Here is a neat little mystery to puzzle your friends.

Effect

While your back is turned a friend takes a pencil that has an eraser on one end and rolls it up tightly in a piece of opaque paper (*see photo 1*). He either twists the ends to secure them or sellotapes them (*see photo 2*). He then turns the paper-covered pencil around a number of times in his hand so no one can know which end is which.

You now turn round and take the pencil in your right hand and hold it up for all to see. Putting your left fingertips to your left temple in the time-honoured fashion much favoured by magicians when performing mental magic, you suddenly announce that you are 100 per cent certain that the point of the pencil is pointing to the right. Carefully you unwrap the pencil to reveal that it is indeed so.

Secret

When you take the paper-wrapped pencil, hold it between your right thumb and first finger at the exact centre of the pencil, then slowly relax your grip until you feel one end of the pencil tilt fractionally downwards (*see photo 3*). That will be the end with the eraser so you will know the opposite end is the point and you can announce its direction. The real trick, within the trick, in

1

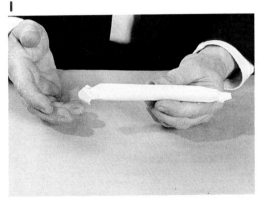

2

3

performance is to gain vital information without the spectators being aware of it, so make the most of your psychic presentation. Of course, the reason the eraser end of the pencil always tilts downwards is that it is heavier than the point end. On such simple knowledge are good tricks built.

The X-Rated Psychic

Using the same pencil from the last trick you proceed to perform a really baffling mystery.

EFFECT

The Psychic Wonder Worker (that's you, remember) gives a friendly helper a pack of cards and asks him to shuffle the cards thoroughly, keeping them face down so you cannot know the position of any of the cards. He is then instructed to hold the cards behind his back, keeping them face down and cut them as many times as he likes. When he is satisfied you give him a pencil and ask him to mark the back of the top card with a large X. He is to do this behind his back so even he has no idea which card he has marked. When he has completed this task you ask for the return of the pencil and further instruct him to cut the cards, behind his back, as many times as he likes, again until he is satisfied. When he indicates he is, you ask him to bring them from behind his back and place them face down, neatly squared, on the table.

You then ask him if he has any idea which card he marked? He can only answer no, and yet you say that your psychic vibes are suggesting a red card, a low-value spot card, a heart, yes, you are certain it is the 2 of Hearts. Will he look through the pack to verify the truth of this psychically induced statement? He does so and there is only one card in the entire pack that is marked in pencil with a large X. It is the 2 of Hearts!

SECRET

The method that makes this trick possible is incredibly cunning and should provide you with an insight into the devious, almost lateral, thinking that magicians apply when creating effects. Before you read any further, put this book down and try to work out the trick method that makes the effect, as presented, possible. I'll give you two clues. You supply the pack of cards and you supply the pencil.

If you have arrived at a solution that can work, given the conditions of the effect, well done! The secret of this trick is that the pencil doesn't write. If you wear the point of a soft lead pencil down so that it writes quite thickly, and then coat the semi-blunt point (but not the wood surround) with some clear nail varnish (borrowed from Mum), when dry the pencil will not transfer lead graphite to paper. But it will look to anybody, not in the know, just like an ordinary pencil. And that is the beauty of the secret. A pencil, especially in a classroom, is such an ordinary, everyday object, that it just does not create suspicion. The fact that you may have used it in the previous trick psychologically misdirects the spectators' thoughts away from any suspicion regarding the pencil.

The other subtlety in the method is that you earlier, secretly, marked the back of the 2 of Hearts with a large, thick, pencilled cross, such as your gimmicked pencil would apparently have made. For clarity we have used a felt-tip marker pen in the photograph. This suggests another subtle notion. Instead of giving the spectator a pencil to mark the card, give him a felt-tip pen that has dried out. He'll never know. This could also be used if you should ever be requested to perform the trick for people who have seen you do it before using a pencil.

In performance you make sure that nobody else looks at the cards as your helper marks the back of the card behind his back. The reason you give is that nobody

should be able to give you any clues or let you know the name of the card that was supposedly marked. Perform the effect as explained earlier, be strong and positive in your presentation and you will have acquired a powerful trick that will fool adults as well as your friends.

Two further points to think about are that it is worthwhile to have a second identical pencil, that you haven't gimmicked, which you can switch in your pocket for the one used in the trick. And, of course, you won't repeat the trick for the same group of spectators. If, at a later date, you do show it to friends who may have seen it before make sure you have marked a different card.

Predictable

Here is a very mysterious mind-reading trick that will puzzle anybody's little grey cells.

*E*FFECT

The magician places a sealed envelope on the table. Drawn on the front of the envelope is a large question mark. Next to the envelope the magician places a pack of cards, face down. Two dice are now rolled on to the table by the magician who explains that nobody can predict what numbers will be uppermost, on top of the dice, when they are shaken and rolled. It is a truly random way of arriving at different combinations of numbers.

Handing the dice to a spectator the magician asks him, or her, to shake the dice in his cupped hands and then roll them on to the table. The dice roll to a stop. The magician asks if the spectator is satisfied that the top numbers of the dice were arrived at freely and were not in any way influenced by the magician. He gives

the spectator a choice – he can stay with the uppermost numbers or he can shake and roll the dice again, it is the spectator's decision. Whether the spectator stays or rolls again, the magician asks the spectator to add the two top numbers of the dice together. For example, we'll say the

numbers are 5 and 5 which, added together, equal 10.

'Now,' says the magician. 'If the top numbers were arrived at random then so were the bottom numbers, so please add those together.' The spectator turns the dice over and adds

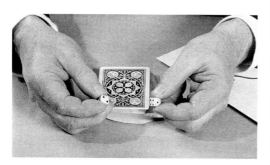

the bottom numbers together; in this case, these add up to 4. 'Now add 4 and 10 together, please,' says the magician. The spectator does so and the total equals 14. 'Well, now having arrived at a random number, I would

like you to pick up the pack of cards from the table, turning them face up as you go, and stop at the fourteenth card, your random number.'

The spectator deals the cards face up, stopping at the fourteenth card. It is the 4 of Spades. 'Please open the envelope.' The spectator does so,

removing a piece of paper on which is written:

'I predict the four of Spades!'

Secret

Before you perform this trick place the 4 of Spades at the fourteenth position down from the top of the face-down pack. Then write, 'I predict the four of Spades' on a piece of paper, fold it in half and seal it in an envelope (you fold it so that it can't be read through the envelope). Then draw a nice, bold, mysterious question mark on the front of the envelope. Get two dice, and you're ready to go. Perform the trick as it is presented above and you can't go wrong. But, remember you must only perform this trick once before the same group of spectators. The real secret of the trick is that the top and bottom numbers of any die (the singular of dice), will always add up to 7, so two dice will always add up to 14. Not a lot of people know that!

Cut the Cards

Whenever magicians meet to discuss things magical, they often refer to the 'principle' of the trick. What they are referring to is the basic method which makes a trick work. Here is a trick that uses a simple, but very effective, principle.

Effect

A spectator freely selects and remembers a card which is returned to the centre of the pack. The magician hands the pack to the spectator and instructs him to cut the pack five times, not four, not six, but exactly five cuts, thus completely losing the card somewhere in the pack. Taking the pack back, the magician asks the spectator to concentrate on his card whilst he looks through the pack. The magician then places one card face down on the table and asks the spectator to name the card he is thinking of; he does so and is told to turn over the card on the table. It is the selected card!

Secret

The method, or principle, that makes this trick work is called the Key Card principle. Here's what happens. Ask a spectator to shuffle the pack and hand it back to you; hold it face down in your left hand. Ask him or her if they know how to cut the cards. Demonstrate this as you ask the question by cutting off half the pack and, as you gesture when talking, secretly glance at the bottom card of the pack in your right hand and place the pack on the table. Then complete the cut by putting the cards in your left hand on top of those on the table. In this way you now know the bottom card of the pack; this is your Key Card. Do make sure that you look at it very casually, so that the spectator doesn't realise what you've done.

Now tell the spectator that he is going to select a card in a most random way. Pick up the pack and, holding it in your left hand, begin by cutting off small stacks of cards and placing them face down on top of each other in a pile on the table. Tell him to stop you any time he likes as you continue cutting off small stacks on to the pile on the table. When he does so, ask him to look at the top card of the pile on the table, remember it, and place it back on the pile on the table. Then drop all the cards from your left hand on to the pile on the table and square up the pack. Your Key Card is now on top of his selected card.

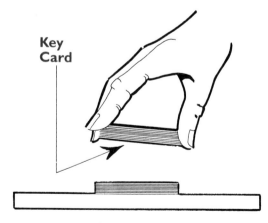

Key Card

Now ask him to pick up the pack and cut it exactly five times. This is really misdirection which takes his attention away from what has happened. When he has completed five cuts, take the pack and look through it.

What you are looking for is your remembered Key Card. When you find it, the card to its immediate right, i.e., below it, will be his selected card. Take it out and put it face down on the table. Occasionally, when you take the pack from a spectator to look through it for your Key Card, you will see the card on the face of the pack. When this happens, immediately put the pack face down on the table and ask him to press his thumb down on the pack and then turn over the top card. It will be his card!

The Magician Predicts

The Key Card principle is taken a step further in this clever version of a mental magic trick.

Effect

A pack of cards is shuffled by a spectator. Taking the cards the Great One flips through them and removes any Jokers, claiming they interfere with his mental powers. He puts the cards on the table and, with a pencil and notepad in hand, tells a girl in the audience that he is going to make an accurate prediction, foretelling something she is about to do, and to prove it is not a coincidence he will do it twice. Gazing at her for a second he writes something on his notepad, tears off one page, folds it up, puts it on the table and covers it with an upturned tumbler.

'That is my first prediction,' he states. He then hands the pack to the girl and asks her to think of a number; then, when he turns his back, she is to deal cards one at a time on top of each other, face down in a pile equal to the number she is thinking of. If, for example, she is thinking of the number 13 she will deal that number of cards. When she has done this she is to look at and remember the thirteenth card dealt, then turn it face down on the pile on the table, pick up the pile and put it back on to the pack she is holding and cut the cards once, burying the chosen card in the middle of the pack.

The magician turns round and takes the pack. He now studies another spectator (this time a boy) for a second. Then he runs through the pack, looking at the faces of the cards to see which card suggests itself for the next prediction. Satisfied, he puts the cards on the table, picks up his pencil and notepad and writes another prediction which he tears off, folds up and places under the tumbler with the first prediction.

He turns his back again and asks the girl to whisper the number she chose to the boy, who is instructed to deal that number of cards, one at a time face down in a pile on the table, and look at and remember the last card. When he has done this, he is to reassemble the pack and shuffle it.

The magician turns around, lifts up the tumbler and hands one slip of paper to the girl and the other to the boy. He asks the girl to name her chosen card; she calls the 6 of Clubs. The boy, similarly requested, calls out the Jack of Diamonds. Each is now requested to open their slips of paper.

On the girl's is written:
THE MAGICIAN PREDICTS SHE WILL CHOOSE THE 6 OF CLUBS. On the boy's is written:
THE MAGICIAN PREDICTS HE WILL CHOOSE THE JACK OF DIAMONDS.

SECRET

Two subtleties make this super trick possible. When the magician removes the Joker from the pack, having previously made sure there was one in the pack, he remembers two Key Cards, the top card and the bottom card. He then writes his first prediction, the name of the top card of the pack. (Although apparently writing the girl's prediction he actually writes the

boy's prediction.) This is folded up and put under the upturned tumbler. The girl is now given the pack and does exactly as described in the Effect, which will leave her selected card under the second Key Card, formerly the bottom card in the pack.

When the magician looks through the pack for the second time he finds the second Key Card, the former bottom card, and, noting the card beneath it, he cuts the pack at this point, bringing it to the top and the second Key Card to the bottom again.

He now writes his second prediction, apparently the boy's (but really the girl's) and writes down the name of the card which he noted, now the top card of the pack. This prediction is folded and put under the tumbler – but remember which one it is, remember its position.

The girl whispers her number to the boy, who deals down that many cards and remembers the last one, then reassembles the pack. Finish as explained in the Effect. But, and this is what makes the trick, when you take the folded predictions from under the glass make sure you give the girl her prediction and the boy his. Don't make a big move of it, do it casually and don't draw attention to it whilst you patter about the possibility of your predictions coming true. Then you finish the trick as described.

This is not an easy trick to explain in print. The way to learn it is to practise a number of times until you become familiar with the sequence of moves. It may seem strange at first, it will feel like there is a lot to remember; there isn't, really, and familiarity will breed mastery. Then you will appreciate the subtle logic of the method and will have added a very strong effect to your repertoire.

KEY

2nd Prediction

7

Party Pieces

The wonderful thing about magic as opposed to any other branch of entertainment is that it is interactive. With most of the things you see on TV you play a passive role – you look and, hopefully appreciate. But magic challenges you. It fools your eye and baffles your brain. It defies logic, and never more so than when you participate in the tricks. The effects in this chapter are all designed for your friends' participation. So why not invite your friends round for tea and magic? Throw a magic party! But remember, not before your practice in private has made you master of your magic.

The Magic Tree and the Magic Ladder

Here are two very pretty effects that need a minimum of preparation and will put to good use a pile of old newspapers or old comics.

THE MAGIC TREE EFFECT

The magician demonstrates the ancient art of paper tearing. Taking a rolled-up newspaper he makes three tears and proceeds to pull the centre of the newspaper roll out until he is holding a tall paper tree.

SECRET

Four sheets of tabloid-size newspaper are glued together along the edges by overlapping the ends about 1 to 2 inches

Glue

The No News
FOR EVERY DAY OF THE YEAR
HEADLINE MAGIC
for
GIRLS AND
BOYS

(3–5cms). If, after glueing, you laid this newspaper strip on the floor it would be about 8 feet (2$\frac{1}{2}$ metres) long, which is a clue as to why this is such an effective entertainment. Now roll this newspaper strip into a tube as you glue the sheets of newspaper together. This can be done on a table. Don't roll it too tightly, the diameter of the finished tube should be about 2 inches (5cms). When you have finished rolling put an elastic band or strip of sellotape around the lower half of the roll to secure it. Now, very carefully, cut down along the length of the tube to about half

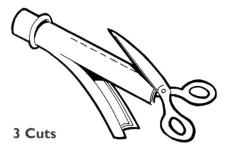

3 Cuts

its length. Turn the tube round a little and make a second similar cut. And repeat a third time. This will give you a tube cut half along its length in three equal segments. Now take a spare page of newspaper, roll this page around the cut portion of the newspaper roll and glue the edge. This disguises the preparation that you have made.

To present the Magic Tree, pick up the prepared roll of newspaper and tell the spectators that you are going to attempt an unusual feat of paper tearing. Now tear down, with both hands, along the already cut lines. These will act as a guide to tearing the paper as straight as possible.

Open out, by pushing back the three strips, and begin to pull the centre of the roll out. Tighten the roll by twisting the stalk after each pull. Continue pulling the tree upwards as far as it will go without falling over. I won't tell you how tall your tree will finally be, I'll let you find out for

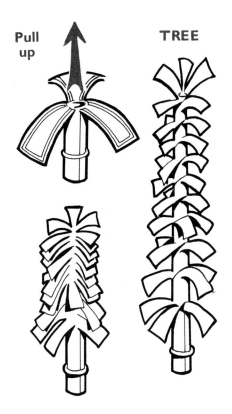

Pull up

TREE

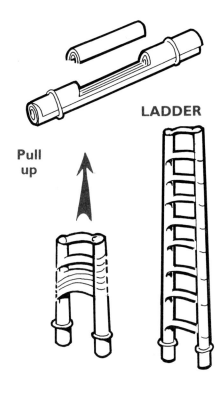

Pull up

LADDER

yourself. All I will say is, you are in for a surprise! After the Magic Tree you present the Magic Ladder.

THE MAGIC LADDER EFFECT

Taking a rolled-up newspaper the magician tears out part of its centre and pulls out a paper ladder.

SECRET

Prepare a roll of newspaper by glueing and rolling exactly as you did in the Magic Tree. Secure this roll with two elastic bands, one at each end. Now make two cuts into the roll, as though you were dividing the tube into three equal-length pieces. The cuts should go halfway into the thickness of the tube, not deeper than the centre of the roll. Now cut out the centre section of the tube along its length between the two

earlier cuts. Take one page of newspaper and roll it around and glue it, so that the tube looks just like a tube of newspaper. The preparation is then hidden.

To present, simply tear out, with your hands, the centre section of outer paper. Bend back each tube end and start to pull out the centres of each end, a little at a time. Slowly the rungs of your ladder will appear. Keep extending the ladder until it reaches its full length. How long is that? You'll have to find out for yourself. But don't be surprised if it's taller than you!

Like all the tricks in this book, practise the Magic Tree and the Magic Ladder until you've got the hang of making and presenting them, and you'll get a lot of fun out of them.

One final word: be very careful with the scissors. I only want you to cut the paper, not yourself.

The Can't-See Miracle

This trick is unusual in that most of it takes place in a completely darkened room.

EFFECT

A spectator is given a pack of cards to hold. The magician turns off the light and feels his way to the spectator so that he is in touching distance. The room should be in total darkness at this point. The magician instructs the spectator to shuffle the cards as much as he likes, only stopping when he wants to. Then he is to remove any card from the pack and put it on the magician's outstretched hand. It's impossible to see anything and yet the magician states, 'I believe your freely chosen card is the 3 of Hearts.'

The spectator turns on the light, there is one card face down on the magician's hand. The magician offers it to the spectator who turns it over to reveal the 3 of Hearts!

SECRET

This is a pretty sneaky secret. Prior to the performance you take the 3 of Hearts out of the pack and put it into your jacket pocket. You perform the trick as described and, as the spectator goes to turn the light back on, you simply swap the card on your hand for the 3 of Hearts in your pocket. You make sure that, when the light is switched back on, the 3 of Hearts is face down on your outstretched hand. A bit of acting will help here; blink your eyes a little at the sudden light as you offer the card for the spectator to turn over and confirm your prediction.

Magicopter

Here is a bit of fun with paper. The best type of paper for this is a stiff, cartridge-type paper, or even a piece of very thin card. You will also need a paperclip.

HOW TO MAKE IT

To make the Magicopter, measure out with a ruler and pencil, and cut carefully (mind your fingers), a piece of paper 9 inches by 2 inches (23cms × 5cms). Now carefully measure and mark the paper exactly as illustrated. Then cut a straight line from the top, between A and B, as far as the dotted line at X. Then make two smaller cuts at point Y.

Now you are ready to make your folds. D is folded in, then C is folded over it. Be sure to make sharp creases using your thumbnail or the edge of a ruler. Now fold E up and over F. Then fold A and B in opposite directions at point X, and secure E and F with the paperclip.

You are now ready to launch your Magicopter. Stand on tiptoe, hold the Magicopter in your hand so that the blades A and B are uppermost. Stretch your arm up and lightly throw your Magicopter into the air. Watch it spin round and round as it falls to the ground. Obviously, the higher up you launch it the better it will spin.

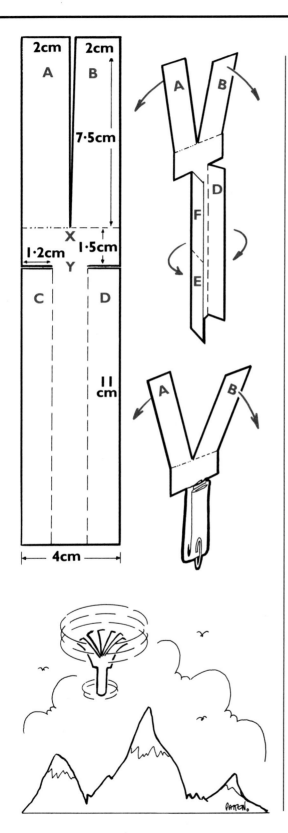

Abracadabra Spell

Here is another of those spelling card tricks that works by itself, with just a little help from you.

Effect

Just by following the instructions listed under Secret you are going to baffle yourself. But you will also be able to baffle other people.

Secret

Spread the cards out so they are facing you. Pick out any two spot cards between Ace and 9.

Put one face up to your left, the other face up to your right.

Hold the pack face down in your hands. Deal on to the card on your left enough cards to add up to ten, e.g., for a face-up three-spot card deal seven cards to bring it up to ten. Do the same with the card on your right. Now add together the values of your two original spot cards and deal that number of cards face down into another pile. Secretly look at the top card of those still in your hands and remember it. Gather up all the cards from the table and put them all face down on top of the cards in your hand. Now deal one card for each letter of the words **MAGIC CIRCLE**. Now deal one card from the pack for each letter of the magic word **ABRACADABRA**. Turn over the top card of those left in your hand. Surprised?

Bungling Burglars

Tricks that have an interesting story are always popular. Here is a classic effect in which a story is actually the basis of the trick.

Effect

The magician places one card face down on the table, without showing its face, to the right. He then takes four cards from the top of the pack and places the pack face down in the centre of the table. He now shows the faces of the four cards he is holding. They are the four Jacks which he calls the Bungling Burglars. He then tells the story of four burglars who went to rob a house. They climbed up the fire escape at the back of the house to the roof (the four Jacks are squared up and the pile is placed face down on top of the pack). One burglar, the first one, went to the basement of the house (the top Jack is put face down into the pack, towards the bottom). The second burglar went to the first floor of the house (the next Jack is put face down into the pack, in the middle). The third burglar went to the third floor (the third Jack is put face down into the pack towards the top). And the fourth burglar stayed on the roof of the house to act as a lookout (the fourth Jack is turned face up on top of the pack).

And so the burglars were busy burgling the house when, suddenly, the lookout burglar saw a policeman coming (the magician turns the card to the right, face up, on the table. It is a Joker). Quickly he called to the other burglars to come up to the top of the house to make their getaway down the fire escape at the back of the building (the top Jack is put on the table, to the left of the pack, face up). Then, the second burglar arrived on the roof and escaped (the new top card is turned face up – it is a Jack! It is put face up, to the left of the pack). Then the third burglar arrived on the roof and escaped (the top card is turned face up – another Jack! It is put face up, to the left of the pack). Finally, the fourth burglar arrived on the roof and escaped (the top card is turned over, it is the last Jack! It is put with the other Jacks). When the policeman arrived at the house (the Joker is placed face up on top of the pack), it was too late, the burglars had escaped. But they had left all their loot behind, which just goes to prove that crime doesn't pay!

Secret

The pack needs to be set up in the following way. Hold the pack face down then put the four Jacks face down on top of the pack. Then, on top of the four Jacks, put three more cards, it doesn't matter what they are, and on top of those put a Joker. So, from the top of the pack, face down, the set-up is as follows: Joker, three indifferent cards, four Jacks and the rest of the pack.

Now, as you tell your story, here's what you do. Put the top card (the Joker or, if you haven't got one, the Ace of Clubs, the policeman) face down to the right. Then, without reversing their order, push off the seven top cards, under cover of your fingers, and keep them squared up in a pile as you put the rest of the pack face down on the table (this is the house). Now show the face cards of the pile you are holding in your right hand and, very carefully with your left fingers, spread the cards so that the four Jacks can be seen (see photo 1). But, equally carefully, keep the other three cards hidden behind the four Jacks as you introduce the Jacks as the Bungling Burglars (see photo 2). Practise this bit of handling in a mirror so that you can see what your audience will see, until you can safely spread seven cards as four. Then you square the cards up and put the four burglars (really seven cards) on top of the pack. Now it should be obvious to you that, when you put the first burglar to the bottom of the pack, and the second and third burglars into the pack, it is really the three indifferent cards that are going into the pack.

1

2

Turn the last burglar (the top Jack), face up. This is the lookout. From here you progress as detailed under the Effect. This is a very good little trick that people love. Go to it, and do it!

Mirror Mirror

This seldom-seen trick relies on two secret principles to achieve its mystery.

EFFECT

The magician places a hand-mirror face down on the table. He then asks a spectator to write down on a piece of paper any three numbers of his choice, provided the first and third numbers differ by no less than 2. For example, let's say he writes 229. Tell him to reverse the order of the number and subtract the smaller number from the larger, e.g.,

$$\begin{array}{r} 922 \\ -\underline{229} \\ 693 \end{array}$$

Then he must reverse the numbers in this answer and add them together, e.g.,

$$\begin{array}{r} 693 \\ +\underline{396} \\ 1089 \end{array}$$

The magician picks up the hand-mirror and holds it in front of the spectator's face so he can see his reflection in it, and intones,

> 'Mirror, mirror in my hand,
> Who's the greatest magician in the land?'

'Of course, this is a silent mirror,' says the magician. 'But it does work, just breathe heavily on to the mirror.'

The spectator does so and, as the mirror mists up, he clearly sees the number 1089 appear on the misted glass!

SECRET

You will need to experiment a little to find the best mixture for this. But try a little household detergent or washing-up liquid in a glass of water, just a dash of liquid soap should do it. Mix it up, then dip your finger in it and carefully print on to the glass of the mirror the number 1089. Let the mirror

dry and the number should be invisible but, when you breathe on the glass, it will magically appear. If you present the subtraction and addition sum exactly as described under the Effect, the result will always be the number 1089.

That being the case, it naturally goes without saying that you should only present this trick once to the same audience – so I won't say it!

Ice Magic

We featured this stunt in one of the audience-participation spots in our television magic show.

EFFECT

The challenge issued was to lift an ice cube from a glass of water with nothing but a piece of string. One spectator actually managed to lasso his ice cube and lift it from the water. But he was the exception that proved the rule for millions who couldn't, until we demonstrated the real method.

SECRET

The solution is rooted in basic chemistry. Lay a loop of string, so it rests flat, on top of the ice cube. Then sprinkle ordinary table salt across the string and the ice cube. In a very short time the interaction between the salt and ice will have frozen the string to the ice cube, sufficiently to allow you to lift the cube from the water by the string.

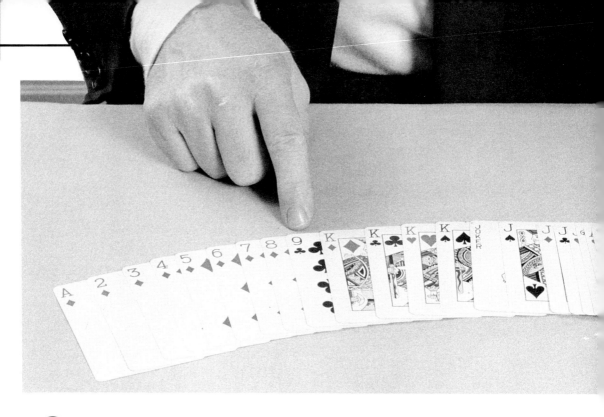

Cards and Numbers

This very effective trick is a good example of the way magicians disguise the secret method by good presentation.

Effect

By dealing cards and adding numbers given to him by a spectator, the magician magically reveals the four Kings.

Secret

What makes this effect work every time is the secret preparation you do beforehand. Prepare the pack so that the 9 of Clubs is the ninth card from the top of the pack and the four Kings are at positions ten, eleven,

twelve and thirteen. Hold the pack face down. Now present the trick in the following manner:

'Let's have a little fun with numbers,' says the magician. 'Give me a number between, say, ten and twenty,' he asks a spectator. He is given the number fourteen. The magician deals fourteen cards, face down in a pile on the table. Putting the rest of the pack aside he picks up the pile from the table.

'Now, fourteen is written as one and four, so let's add them together, which makes five.' He then deals and counts five cards, face down in a pile on the table. He turns the fifth card over to reveal a King, which is put aside. The cards in his hand are dropped on to the pile, just dealt, on the table. The pile is picked up and put on top of the pack.

'Let's do it again. Give me another number between ten and twenty.' This time the number is nineteen. The magician deals nineteen cards, putting the rest of the pack

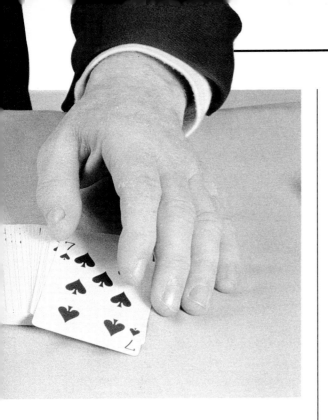

aside. He adds one and nine together. 'Numbers one and nine add up to ten,' he says as he picks up the pile on the table and deals, counting as he goes, ten cards on to the table. The tenth card is turned over to reveal another King, which is put aside with the first King. The cards in his hands are placed on the pile on the table which is then placed on the rest of the pack.

'Give me another number between ten and twenty.' This time the number is seventeen. He deals seventeen cards in a pile on the table, puts the pack aside, picks up the seventeen cards, adds one and seven together, and deals eight cards on to the table, turning up the eighth card to reveal another King.

The cards in his hands are dropped on to the pile on the table which is then placed on to the bulk of the pack.

'Let's try for the last King in a different way,' says the magician as he picks up the pack. 'Let's see if we can get a lucky number,'

he says, as he turns over the top card of the pack. It is a 9. 'Well, look, we've got a 9 card. Let's see if it will do the trick.' He puts the 9 aside and then deals nine cards in a pile on the table, counting as they are dealt. The ninth card is turned over to reveal the last King.

The Uncanny Separation

Once learnt, this super trick is likely to become one of your favourites. It is one of those rare effects that has an additional surprise at the end.

Effect

Taking the pack from its case the magician counts twenty cards into a face-down pile on the table; the rest of the pack is placed aside. Having done this he explains that he is going to make a mess of the cards. Picking up the pile of twenty cards he mixes them up so that some are face up and some are face down, in the following way. He cuts the pile at some random point and turns the two top cards face up. He cuts the pile again and turns another two top cards face up. He repeats this procedure another four or five times.

The magician now hands the pile of cards to a spectator and asks him to hold the cards out of sight under the table. He is instructed to cut the cards under the table; when he has done so he is to take the top card of

the pile and place it on the bottom of the pile. The next top card he is to take off, turn it over, bring it out from beneath the table and place it on the table. The next card from the top of the pile is placed on the bottom of the pile. The next top card is taken off, turned over and placed on the table. The spectator repeats this a few more times. Then he continues again exactly as before. The top card goes to the bottom of the pile. The next top card is taken off, turned over and placed on the table. It is most important that the spectator makes two separate piles on the table, one for those cards that come out from under the table face down, and one for those that come out face up.

After ten cards have been placed in their respective piles on the table, the spectator is instructed to turn over the entire pile he is holding under the table, shuffle it and cut the cards. When he has done so, he starts the procedure as before. The top card goes to the bottom, the next card is turned over and placed on the appropriate pile on the table. The next top card to the bottom. The next is turned over and placed on the table, and so on until there are no cards left.

Now comes the climax when it can be revealed that not only has the spectator separated the face-up cards from the face-down, but all the black cards face one way and all the red cards the other – which is pretty impressive.

SECRET

Before he performs the trick the magician secretly arranged twenty cards in a sequence of alternating colours, first black, then red, then black, then red, and so on. This stack of cards is placed on top of the pack which is put back into the card case.

When he is ready to perform the trick, the magician removes the pack from its case and counts the top twenty cards, one at a time, into a face-down pile on the table. He must be careful not to let anybody catch a glimpse of the faces of the cards. He then goes through the business of cutting the cards, and turning over the top two cards each time. When he has done all this as described under the Effect he can spread the cards and show them, top and bottom, to be thoroughly mixed up. His part of the trick is done and he hands the cards to the spectator who continues the trick as directed.

All the magician has to do is silently to count the number of cards that are dealt on to the piles on the table. When ten cards have been dealt he stops the spectator and has him further mix the cards, as described, before completing the routine until the cards are exhausted. He can then conclude the trick by showing that the spectator has not only separated face-up and face-down cards but, as an added kick, segregated the colours as well.

Despite all the mixing and turning over of cards, the trick works, in case you are puzzled, because there is a related arrangement to the cards all the time. So the end result for the magician and, we hope, for the spectator, will always be a satisfactory one.

8

Grown-Up Magic

One of the greatest moments for a young magician is the first time he or she fools an adult with a magic trick. This chapter gives you eight terrific tricks that will fool grown-ups, provided that you practise them until they're perfect. But don't try to learn them all at once – select one and make it yours, practise until nobody else can do it as well as you can. Only then move on to the next trick.

Here's a story that contains sound advice. In late Victorian early Edwardian England the best magician in the land was David Devant. He was once approached by a young magician who boasted that he could do over a hundred tricks. 'That's very good,' replied Devant, 'I can only do eight. But *I* do them better than anyone else!'

Of course, Devant knew many more tricks than that, but he was making the point that by doing eight tricks better than anyone else he had become the best in the business. Hopefully, *you* will soon become the best in the business.

Fair Exchange

If you really want badly to fool a friend with a card trick, this is the one to do. To the uninitiated it is completely inexplicable; this is another way of saying it is a great trick.

EFFECT

Two packs of cards are used in this effect, preferably with contrasting back designs. The King of Cards (that's you) offers a choice of either pack to the spectator. Each shuffles their respective packs. The packs are exchanged and shuffled again. The packs are exchanged again and both cut their packs a number of times. The packs are exchanged again. Each now takes one face-down card from the pack and looks at it, without the other seeing it. Each card is placed on top of the pack it came from and each pack is cut, then cut again, and cut once again for luck. The packs are exchanged once again and cut once again for even more luck.

'Are you following all this?' asks the magician. No matter what the answer is, he tells the spectator to take his selected card from the pack he is holding, keeping it face down. The magician does the same.

'Are you ready for this?' asks the magician. Again, no matter what the answer is, both cards are turned face up and are seen to be identical!

SECRET

For some reason, people find all the pack exchanging and cutting very amusing, no bad thing for a magic trick. It also distracts their attention away from the simplicity of the method which is the very basic use of our old friend, the Key Card. All the shuffling and cutting means nothing until the last exchange before each selects a card and puts it on top of his pack, then cuts the cards to lose his selected card. What really happens is that you must note and remember the bottom card of your pack at the time when you exchange it for the spectator's pack, just before each selects a

card. So when each of you takes a card and looks at it, and apparently remembers it, the spectator does remember his; you, however, ignore yours.

Each selected card is then placed on top of the packs and the packs are cut. Your Key Card, the bottom card you memorised, is now on top of his selected card. Cutting

Key Card

Spectator's Card

the packs a few more times is just presentational misdirection. The packs are then exchanged again. You now have his pack with your Key Card immediately on top of his selected card. You each cut the cards a couple more times and only then find the selected cards in the pack you are both holding. You look for your Key Card and the card below it will be his selected card which you now pretend is the one you chose. He, of course, is finding the duplicate of that very card.

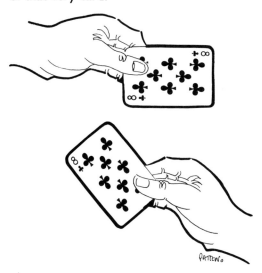

One point to bear in mind when looking for your Key Card is that, if you see it on the bottom of your pack when looking for your (really his) selected card, it simply means his card will be on the top of the pack. What makes this such a strong trick is that you actually take his selected card from the actual pack he selected it from, pretending it is the card you selected. And he takes the identical card from your pack, never realising that you know the card he selected. The end result to him is a miracle of coincidence. To you, it's a very elegant card trick for such a simple principle.

Here are the bare bones of the routine to help you master it:

1 Magician and spectator have a pack each.
2 Both packs are shuffled and exchanged.
3 Both packs are shuffled and exchanged.
4 Both packs are cut a number of times. Magician glimpses and *remembers* the bottom card of his pack. This is his Key Card.
5 Both packs are exchanged. Both take a card from their packs. Spectator memorises his card, puts it on top of his pack and cuts the pack and cuts it again.
6 Magician takes a card, pretends to memorise it (really he promptly forgets it, he has already memorised his Key Card in the spectator's pack). He puts it on top of his cards and cuts the pack once again.
7 Both packs are cut twice more, exchanged, and cut once again.
8 Both look for their selected cards. The magician locates his Key Card. Immediately beneath it is the spectator's card which the magician pretends is the card he selected earlier.
9 The spectator locates his selected card.
10 Both cards are revealed to be the same.

Two final thoughts are that both packs could be supplied by the spectator, making it all the more mysterious. And once you have learned the mechanics of the trick and tried it a few times with spectators, you will be able to play with it, shuffling and exchanging, cutting and exchanging as much or as little as you feel works in performance. Study Paul at work on tv and you will get an object lesson in how to control an audience, how to play it for maximum entertainment. In time you may come to find this the most valuable piece of information in the entire book.

How is it Possible?

This is one of the most puzzling tricks of its type. Well presented, this will fool anybody.

Effect

The magician's wrists are tied together in front of him with a length of ribbon so that approximately 16 inches (40cms) of ribbon is between each wrist. A plastic bangle is handed to the magician who turns his back, for a brief moment, on the spectators. On turning back to face them the bangle is now on the ribbon. The wrists are still securely tied, there simply wasn't time to untie one wrist, put the ribbon through the bangle and retie the ribbon to the wrist. So how is it possible?

Secret

Two identical plastic bangles make this effect possible. Prior to performance one bangle is put over your left hand, over the wrist and then pushed up your forearm so that it firmly grips the arm and won't slide down to your wrist during movement. Put on a jacket, or your school blazer, and you will see how well the sleeve hides the bangle.

To present the trick ask someone to tie each wrist with about a 3 foot (1 metre) length of ribbon. Make sure that no one can see up your left sleeve by bending your elbows so your wrists are in a vertical position as they are being tied.

Now, with your right hand, take the bangle from the person you gave it to at the beginning of the trick. Hold it in the air with a flourish as you say, 'Watch . . .'. Turn your back on the spectators and, as you do, quickly put the bangle inside your jacket and tuck it out of sight into the top of the waistband of your trousers or skirt; then

bend your knees and lean forward as you reach into your left sleeve and pull the bangle down over your wrist and on to the ribbon. Turn back to the spectators, as you say, '. . . and wonder'. Reveal the bangle on the centre of the ribbon.

The effect to aim for is almost one continuous movement as you say, 'Watch and wonder'. It should appear that you have turned away, bent over slightly and straightened up as you turn back to face them. The principle of this is that the larger movements of the body should cover the smaller movements of the hands, thus hiding the working of the trick.

It is a terrific effect and well worth putting in the practice to perfect it. One tip is to try it in front of a mirror so you can see what the spectator should see in performance.

I Won't Even Touch the Cards

This very clever trick, which has been known to baffle experienced magicians, employs a highly unusual principle.

EFFECT

The magician (that's you) gives a pack of cards to a spectator and informs him, 'This is the first and last time I shall handle the pack during this trick; we are going to perform a miracle together, and I won't even touch the cards. OK, I want you to shuffle and cut the pack until you are absolutely certain that neither of us can have the slightest knowledge of the position of even a single card. Are you happy? OK, put the pack face down on the table. Now I want you to cut the pack at any point you like and look at the card on the bottom of those you cut off, and remember it.'

The spectator cuts the pack and notes the bottom card as instructed. The magician gestures for the spectator to replace the cards on top of those on the table. The spectator does this. 'Now I want you to cut the pack two or three times to completely lose your card.' Again, the spectator does as instructed. When he has finished cutting the cards, the magician says, 'I think you'll have to agree that not only have I never touched the cards, but it must be impossible for me to know not only where your card is in the pack, but what it is.' The spectator naturally agrees. And the second he agrees the magician reaches to the pack and cuts off a portion of the cards. He announces the name of the spectator's card as he turns the face of the cards he's cut towards the spectator who will be astonished to see that you have cut directly to his chosen card.

SECRET

You perform the trick exactly as explained under Effect, with one qualification. The real work that makes it happen is done in a single gesture. When the spectator has cut off a block of cards, he looks at and remembers the face card. You then point towards the stack of cards left on the table. In the process of pointing at the cards on the table you drop a few grains of salt on to the back of the top card of the pile. To best understand this, pour a little salt on to the table, or into a saucer, then lightly press the pad of your index finger into the salt. Some grains will stick to your finger. To

dislodge them, rub your thumb across your fingertip. Now, if you combine this with a gesture in which you indicate that he is to replace his cards on to those on the table, the natural gesture is to point towards the cards on the table. And it is that motion that enables you to get some grains on to the cards. If you do it casually, the finger never touches the cards, the downward pointing gesture need never go nearer than 3 or 4 inches (8–10cms) from the pack; your action will never be suspected. Why should it be? It's not a magical move, it is simply a light gesture to indicate what you want him to do next.

To cut to his card is simplicity itself. Press lightly down on the pack and you will feel the block of cards almost slide and break at the right point.

There are other ways of revealing his card. You can pick up the entire pack, put it behind your back and cut the cards, take off the bottom card of the cut portion and bring it out with its back towards the spectator, then say, 'Was your card the [and name it]?' When he confirms that you are correct, turn its face towards him, as you simply say, 'I thought it was.'

A second, more showy way of revealing his card is to pick up the entire pack, carefully place it on the floor and, without too much aggression, tap the side of the cards with your foot. The pack will break at the right place. Bend down, lift up the top portion at the break, and say, 'I guess that's what is meant by putting your foot in it!'

All great tricks come with one major recommendation. Practice . . . !

Paul's Favourite

Of all the card tricks that we perform when asked, this stunning effect is one of a special few that are always done. Avid *Paul Daniels Magic Show* fans will have seen us baffle a studio audience with this very trick. Come to think of it, we probably baffled millions watching at home as well!

EFFECT

A spectator thoroughly shuffles a pack of cards, then gives one half to the magician and keeps the other half for himself. They both turn their backs and each removes and remembers a card from his own half. They turn to face each other, holding half the pack face down in their left hands and their chosen cards face down in their right hands.

The magician gives his card to the spectator and instructs him to push it face down into his half of the pack. Similarly, the magician takes the spectator's card from him and pushes it face down into his half of the pack.

So two cards have been chosen, exchanged and lost in two separate halves of the pack. One chosen card is known only to the spectator, the other chosen card only to the magician. The latter now takes the spectator's half of the pack and puts it, with his own half of the pack, behind his back; he also puts the two halves together. Then, turning so everybody can see him doing it, he cuts the pack twice behind his back.

He then turns and puts the pack face down on the table. 'Not only do we not know what each other's selected cards are, we don't know where they are in the pack. Would that be a fair summary of the situation?' Everybody will, of course, agree.

'OK, then, for the first time we will name our cards. Mine was the 4 of Spades, and yours was the . . . ?'

We will suppose the spectator names the King of Hearts. The magician says the magic word, 'ALAMALAGOOLA. Look and wonder!' So saying, he ribbon spreads the cards across the table to reveal two cards face up in the face-down pack. They are the 4 of Spades and the King of Hearts!

SECRET

The first point to remember is that the magician is not interested in the first card which he removes from his half of the pack. But when he receives half the pack from the spectator and turns his back, this is what he really does. Without anybody seeing he turns the cards face up. He looks at and remembers the top card; it happens to be the 4 of Clubs which he then turns over, leaving it face down on the face-up pile of cards in his left hand. He then takes one card off the bottom and turns it face down, keeping it in his right hand as he turns round to face the spectator who has now turned to face the magician.

The clever thing here is that the

spectator thinks the magician has done exactly the same as he has; it never occurs to him that the face-down cards in the magician's left hand are really face up with a face-down 4 of Clubs on top (held squared up). The card in the magician's right hand, which the spectator takes and puts in his half of the pack, is really a red herring, it will not be the card the magician later names as his. The spectator's selected card is inserted face down into the magician's apparently face-down pile (really face up apart from the 4 of Clubs face down on

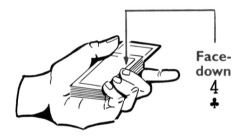

Face-down
4
♣

top), thus reversing it in the pack, along with the 4 of Clubs, when the spectator's half pack is added to the magician's half.

Now here is a crucial move in the trick: when the magician takes the spectator's half pack, he takes it in his right hand and carries it behind his back. At the same time he puts his left hand, plus cards, behind his back; quickly, with one movement, he turns the cards in his left hand over, reversing their

The Turn-over

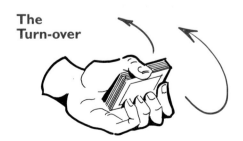

order. Then, without pausing, he turns his back to the spectators so they see him put the cards in his right hand on top of those in his left hand. This is a beautiful move because, not only have you turned the cards in your left hand face down (with the exception of the two chosen cards), the audience sees you add the face-down cards in the right hand to those in the left, thus reinforcing the impression that all the cards are face down.

Now cut the pack twice, the first time quite deeply, taking about two thirds from the top and putting them on the bottom. The second time make a shallow cut, about a quarter of the pack from top to bottom.

By cutting the pack behind his back the magician has further misdirected the spectators into believing the entire pack is face down; this makes the trick so startling when both selected cards are revealed face up in the pack at the end. The magician, of course, has called out the name of the card he reversed earlier as his chosen card (which, in one sense, it was), the one he gave to the spectator being a red herring.

A few tips to bear in mind when performing this trick will ensure its successful conclusion. Use a pack that has a white border on the back so that a face-up card in a face-down pack can't be seen.

Practise putting the cards behind your back, turning the left-hand cards over as soon as the pack is out of sight, then turning your back to the spectators to witness the cutting of the pack, until it becomes almost one continuous movement.

The way to turn over a stack of cards in one hand is as follows: hold the cards face up in your left hand, thumb on one long side, index finger against the short top end and the middle, fourth and little fingers against the other long side. Now bend your left thumb in and under the cards, and lever them upright against the pads of the middle, fourth and little fingers; then revolve the cards over and back into palm with the thumb, at the same time extending the fingers (all but the index). The cards will then fall quite naturally back into the position they were in before the move. Done quickly the cards are almost flipped over; with a little practice the knack will come. It's not a major move so don't flog it, just let it happen and it will be yours.

This is a super trick which is worth the practice to perfect in both handling and presentation; you'll fool many people with this if you do it properly. Don't forget that we have baffled and entertained millions on television with this trick. Maybe, one day, you will too. Now, wouldn't that be magic?

Looks Impossible

You'll have to be careful to control the angles, or sight lines with this trick. The spectators should be face on and at a little distance from the performer.

Effect

Taking a single playing card the magician manages to balance it so it stands upright on its edge. This is no mean feat but he immediately tops that by balancing a plastic tumbler full of water on the upright card!

Secret

There are very few tricks in this book that require much prior preparation; this one does, but the visual effect makes it worthwhile.

Take two playing cards, the 10 of Hearts and a Joker. Fold the Joker in half along its length, the face of the card outwards, and put glue over one half of the face of the card. Now, very carefully, stick it to the back of the 10 of Hearts, making sure the edges of the cards are in perfect alignment. When the glue has dried you'll see that you have made a double card that looks like a single card, but half of the back can open like a flap that will enable you to stand the card upright and balance a glass of water on it. We suggest using a plastic glass as it

will weigh less than a standard glass. In performance, don't make this look too easy; it should look as though you're doing it for real, a delicate feat of balance. To finish the trick, take the glass in one hand and the card in the other, closing the flap with your thumb as you pick them up.

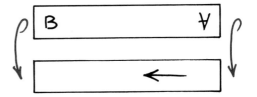

The Famous Afghan Bands

With this strange effect we are going to take a walk through the world of topology, a branch of mathematics that, in this case, explores the properties of single-sided shapes. But, before we get into the meat of the effect and its variations, you may care to explore the underlying principle that is the basis of the trick. You are about to participate in a peculiar puzzle that has been the subject of much speculation and debate, resulting in differing opinions, between scientists and mathematicians.

All you need is a strip of paper $1\frac{1}{2}$ inches by 9 inches (3.8cms × 22.8cms). At the right-hand end ink in an upside-down capital letter A and at the left-hand end ink in a capital B. Turn the paper strip over and ink in an arrow at the right-hand end, pointing from right to left. Now pick up the strip and hold it so that the letters are facing you. Put your left thumbnail over the letter B. Put your right thumb under the strip so that it is on the arrow and your finger will be over the A. Now twist your right hand over so that your right thumbnail is facing upwards. This will give the strip a half twist. Without untwisting the strip, make a circle by placing the letter B on top of the letter A. In this position you can put

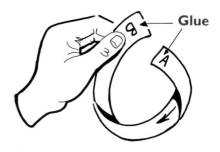

Glue

A on top of B. They will be face to face because the paper strip will be twisted. Now glue A to B. This will give you a circle of paper with a half twist in it, leaving the arrow visible, pointing from your left to right.

You are now ready for your topological trip. Put the tip of your pen on the point of the arrow and draw a continuous line along the centre of the paper strip. You will have to turn the strip as you go and your pen will go out and in and out as you go along until you meet up with the stem of the arrow. Now, here's the curious thing! Although your line has finished where it started, you will see that the line is on both sides of the paper! Now what makes that possible? This question has puzzled mathematicians and scientists. Can you, or your friends, figure it out?

Whilst you're pondering the imponderable, here comes the magic.

EFFECT

The magician steps forward and shows six large loops of paper which are hanging from his left arm; in his right hand are two small pairs of scissors. Taking the paper loops he puts them over his head and hangs them round his neck. Taking one of the loops he hands it out to a spectator, together with a pair of scissors. He requests the spectator to cut the paper loop in the same way as he does. Making a small vertical cut in the centre of the width of his paper band the magician continues to cut down the centre of the paper along its complete length with the intention of dividing the single loop into two separate loops. This the spectator achieves. The magician, however, does the same except that his loops are linked together.

'That's curious,' says the magician. 'You appear to have done it right. I must have taken a wrong turning somewhere. Let's start again.'

He gives the spectator another paper band and takes one for himself. They go through the process of cutting the paper bands as before and end with, in the spectator's case, two single separate loops. The magician now has one giant loop, twice the size of the one he started with.

'Curiouser and curiouser,' says the puzzled magician. 'If I hadn't seen myself cut it, I wouldn't believe it. We will try it one more time.'

He offers the spectator another band of paper and takes one for himself. But, just before they start cutting, he stops the spectator and exchanges his own paper loop for the spectator's one. 'Just to be on the safe side,' he says.

They cut their loops again, and again the spectator succeeds in cutting two single, separate loops. The magician, to his obvious puzzlement, now has a giant loop with a knot in it! This prompts him to say brightly, 'Well, that's enough of that. Anybody want to see a card trick?'

SECRET

You will need to prepare six paper bands. These could either be newspaper strips glued together or paper rolls – such as are used in the tills at supermarket checkouts or in adding machines – these are easily acquired from stationers' shops. The paper must be soft and not too wide.

You will need to decide for yourself which is the best length of paper for you to handle, to present the trick effectively, but all the bands must be the same length at the start. Three of the bands are simply glued together at the ends without twisting the paper at all.

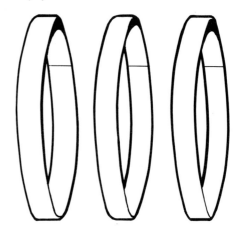

The fourth band is given half a twist then glued, the fifth band is twisted fully round and glued. The sixth is twisted fully round then twisted half again.

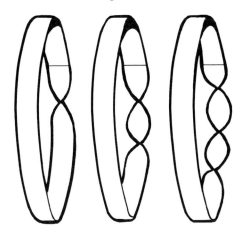

When you drape them over your neck you will have, in the following order:

1 Normal loop, given to the spectator.

2 Half-twist loop, used by the magician.

3 Normal loop, given to the spectator.

4 Full-twist loop, used by the magician.

5 Full-twist-and-a-half loop, given to the spectator.

6 Normal loop, retained by the magician; he then changes his mind and exchanges it for the spectator's loop.

You could reverse this sequence and have the spectator fail each time. But it is probably safer for the magician to fail; plus, there is humour in this approach as well as an extremely puzzling effect.

Up the Garden Path

Finding a selected card after it has been lost in the pack is a basic feat of card magic. Most people have seen, at one time or another, a trick of this type. What is so very effective about this version is that the spectators are given to believe that the magician has made a mistake which they are aware of and he isn't. Needless to say, the magician ultimately triumphs but not before he has led the spectators a merry dance up the garden path.

Effect

A shuffled pack of cards is placed on the table. The magician informs his audience that a card will be freely selected and lost in the pack in the following manner. A spectator is told to cut the pack into three piles, then he is to take a card from the top of one of the piles, show it to the other spectators to help him remember it (the magician discreetly looks away at this point), then place it back on top of any pile, it doesn't have to be the same one, it's up to him. When he has replaced it, he re-assembles the pack by stacking the piles into one complete pack. He may then cut the pack as many times as he likes until he is completely satisfied that his selected card is lost in the pack, certainly to the extent that the magician (who doesn't know what the selected card is at this time) couldn't know where it is.

Taking the pack the magician speaks directly to the person who selected the card, and says, 'I am going to find your card in a very unusual way. I have absolutely no idea what your card is and yet I believe you are going to tell me what it is, without ever saying a word. Puzzled? Well, you've heard of lie detectors, they use them in America to test whether a person is telling the truth or is lying. The theory is that, when a person lies, his body reacts. His pulse rate quickens, tension rises, etc., sufficiently to cause a polygraph machine, to which he is linked, to register this variation in the body's normal pattern. This is the give-away. Whilst I haven't got a polygraph machine I think your body language will give you away. I think I will detect some reaction, no matter how small, either in your expression or your stance, when I come to your card. The challenge for you is to give me no visual clue whatsoever when I come to your card. Yet I'm so confident that I can read you, I guarantee I will find your card. Are you ready? Here we go.'

The magician takes one long, last look at the spectator's face and begins to deal the cards face up into a loose pile on the table. In order for you clearly to understand what happens next we will suppose the spectator chose the 3 of Spades. The magician continues dealing the cards face up on to the pile, looking at each card, then at the spectator in turn, looking at the next card, then the spectator, and so on. He deals the next card, the 7 of Diamonds, looks at the spectator, deals another, the Jack of Hearts, then another, the 5 of Clubs, then another, the Ace of Spades, another, the 3 of Spades, then another card, the 5 of Diamonds, another card, the 9 of Diamonds, another, the 10 of Clubs. Suddenly he pauses, peeks at the top, face-down card in his hand, and says, 'I have an overwhelming feeling that the next card I turn over is your card. And the look on your face will tell me I'm right.'

The spectators will love this moment because they all know that you have already dealt the selected card, the 3 of Spades, on to the face-up pile of cards on the table. They can even see it partially sticking out of the pile. They will almost bet on your being wrong. But you'll be right because, instead of turning over the top card in your hand, you reach down, pull out the 3 of Spades from the face-up pile and turn it over so it's face down!

SECRET

You have, of course, led the spectators right up the garden path in the way you have presented the effect. The presentation completely misdirects them away from the fact that you have totally controlled events. The method is as simple as can be. After the pack has been shuffled all you need to find out is the name of the card on the bottom of the pack; for example, we'll use the Ace of Spades. The pack is face down on the table and a spectator cuts it into three approximately equal piles, looks at the top card of any pile, remembers it, shows it to the other spectators (the more people who see it the better) who will help the build-up at the end. He can replace it on top of any pile. You, of course, have remembered which pile has the Ace of Spades on the bottom. If he places his card (for example, we'll use the 3 of Spades), on the pile with the Ace of Spades on the bottom, instruct him to cut the pile, complete the cut, place the pile on a second pile and then place the remaining pile on top.

If he places the 3 of Spades on a pile that doesn't have the Ace of Spades on the bottom, tell him to pick up the pile that does and drop it on top of the pile on which he placed his selected card. Then lift up half the remaining pile and put the balance of the pack on to those on the table, then put the rest on top, like making a sandwich. He can then cut the complete pack as many times as he likes.

Now you get into your patter about lie detectors and facial reactions, etc. Then you start dealing cards, one at a time face up; when you see the Ace of Spades (this will be your old friend the Key Card), you will know that the next card is the selected card. Just turn it over and continue dealing until another six or seven cards have passed (see photo 1). Announce that the next card you turn over will be the selected card. The audience will think that you mean the top card of those in your left hand. Reach down and turn the 3 of Spades face down on the table (see photo 2).

An amusing aspect of this presentation is

that, while you have apparently gone to great pains to caution them not to react, it is actually you that must control your reactions. When dealing the cards, do it in a uniform, rhythmic way. Don't give them the slightest hint that you know what the card is. It's one of the great fun tricks of magic! Paul has conned, in the nicest possible way, thousands of people with this classic bit of kidology. May you do so as well.

1

2

Miracle Cut and Restored

You can't really claim to be a magician unless you can cut and restore something successfully. As it is our intention to make your introduction to magic the best there is, we naturally included one of the best cut-and-restored tricks you could wish to find.

EFFECT

The magician threads a length of thin string, about 14 inches (35cms) long, through an ordinary drinking straw (see photo 1) so the ends of the string are hanging out of each end of the straw (see photo 2). Bending the straw in half, at its centre, the magician cuts right through the straw and the string with a pair of sharp scissors. And yet, as he straightens the straw and pulls the two halves apart, the string is seen to be in one, undamaged piece!

SECRET

What a clever secret this is! Who would suspect that, in secret, before performing the trick the magician had taken a very sharp knife or razor blade (he had taken it with his Dad's permission and, because he was clever, even asked his Dad to help him) and had made a single cut in the middle of the straw about 2 inches (5cms) in length (see photo 3). The idea is to try to make the cut in such a way that, when the straw is bent in half, so is the slit. As an example, with a

1

2

3

straw 8 inches (20cms) long, the slit would run between inches 3 and 5 (centimetres 7·5 and 12·5). It makes sense to use a ruler to help make the cut in the right place.

A paper straw is probably better for the trick, but a plastic straw is easier to cut. These days, some straws are covered in paper wrappers for reasons of hygiene, especially those found in fast-food restaurants, and, if you are a thinking magician, it might occur to you to acquire some of these straws and carefully open one end of the sealed wrapper, remove the straw and make the slit, then put it back in the wrapper and reseal the end with a dab of glue. This would mean that, without drawing specific attention to it when you perform, psychologically your audience will automatically assume it to be an ordinary (therefore unprepared) straw. As a magician, you have to fool their minds as well as their eyes.

Present the trick exactly as described under Effect, up to the point where the string is in the straw which is bent in half, meaning it is bent double, allowing you to hold it nearer the ends in your left hand (see *photo 4*). Grip both ends of the string, which are hanging from the ends of the straw, with your right fingers, point the bent middle of the straw towards your audience and sharply pull the string towards your body. You will feel the string pull through the slit in the straw and stop at the end of the slit; this should take a split second. You cover this tugging action partly with your left hand, which is in front of your right, and partly by turning half right and reaching over to pick up the scissors from the table to your right. The magical thinking here is that, if you were to pull the string while you were standing still, the movement of your right arm would be noticed by the audience. But if you make 'the move' whilst the whole body is in motion, for the logical reason of picking up the scissors, the larger movement (the body) covers the smaller movement (the arm) and suspicions will not be aroused.

You can now cut the straw at the point at which it is bent by cutting through the bend above the string. The string will be safely out of the cutting area. Put the scissors back on the table, say your

favourite magic word as you cast a shadow over the bent straw with a mystic pass of your right hand, straighten the straw (*see photo 5*) and slowly pull the two halves apart to reveal the restored string (*see photo opposite*).

5

This is a terrific pocket trick and worth practising to achieve a smooth and easy handling. And handling in magic, meaning the way you go about doing a trick, is very important. If, for example, you weren't using a table then you would have the scissors in the top pocket of your jacket, so you would make the crucial pulling move as you look down at your pocket. You would look, grip the straw forward with your left hand and, at the same moment, pull with the right. Immediately, without stopping, continue the right-hand movement up to the pocket to take the scissors, having let go of the string. To the audience it will appear that you moved your left hand forward to make room for the right hand to reach up to the pocket for the scissors.

Always remember that the audience doesn't know what you are going to do, so you 'stage' your handling, you arrange your handling to cover the danger moments when you have to make the secret move.

We continually fool millions of people on television by doing this. The idea is to use the whole body, even the way you walk, in the quest for perfection. Test different ideas, analyse reactions. Keep the audience amused and they will miss your secret moves. This is no accident, so work to your strengths. Equally, don't draw attention to things when you don't need to. If you were to pick up the straw and say, 'I have here an ordinary drinking straw, look, you can see there is nothing in it,' what do you think the audience reaction will be? I'll bet you, they'll be thinking, 'I'd like to have a closer look at that straw.' You would make them wonder when it wasn't necessary.

It is far better to pick up the straw, tear the end off the paper wrapper, slide it a third of the way down the straw, blow through the straw so the wrapper flies off, pick up the string and say, 'String,' as you hold up the string, then lower it and raise the straw as you say, 'Straw.' Then do it again in reverse, saying, 'Straw, string.' Now run it together, 'String, straw … straw, string.' Thread the string through the straw as you say 'String through straw.' Hold it up so they can all see; the slit in the straw will, at all times, be towards you, won't it! Now say, in a deep voice, 'He bends the straw.' Exaggerate this as though you were trying, and failing, to bend a solid iron bar, arms shaking with strain, and slowly it starts to bend, more strain, finally you succeed! You might even get some applause at this point. If you do, take a bow, pulling the string part down the straw as you do (good magicians think on their feet, they take advantage

of any opportunity). If not, carry on as planned, say, 'With no thought of the cost [reach for the scissors] he cuts the straw and the string with a single practised snip.' As you do so, yell at the top of your voice and jump in the air, then look towards the back of the audience and say apologetically, 'Sorry, I didn't mean to wake you up.' Put the scissors away, get serious again and, as you wave your hand over the straw, say dramatically, 'He cast a shadow over the straw and it came to pass that his audience was so amazed to see he had restored the string to useful life as a single length that it burst into long and spontaneous applause.' As you are doing this, wave your hand over the straw, straighten it out and pull both halves apart to reveal the string. Time what you are doing to coincide with the last word as you hold your arms at head height, then drop them and take a bow. You'll find they'll applaud. After all, you have just asked them to or, more to the point, you have directed them to.

How you work an audience is all part of the handling we were talking about earlier. Study Paul's show on television and see how it's done. Then do it your way, don't try to imitate. Learn from the show, instead, and become good at magic.

And, as mentioned earlier, don't 'overprove'. Here's an example. The late, great comedian Eric Morecambe used to perform a funny gag with a paper bag. He would walk on to the stage holding a brown paper bag in his left hand. His thumb was at the back of the bag and his fingers were inside so that the mouth of the bag gaped open and was facing upwards. He would reach into the bag and take out a ball; it was invisible but you knew it was a ball because his right hand was in the shape of a hand holding a ball. He would throw the ball into the air in an arc from right to left; you knew it was right to left because his head moved in an arc as he followed its flight with his eyes. At the split second his eyes met the paper bag, held out at an angle to catch the ball, there would be a sharp, brief, crumpled, snapping sound of impact as he caught the ball in the bag. Visually, the

bag would drop a few inches as the weight of the falling ball hit the bag; he would bend his knees at that split second and straighten up. The effect was perfect. It looked exactly like it would look if he had actually used a ball. But if he had come on and shown the paper bag empty half the humour would have gone. He knew he didn't have to prove anything, even though he could have done so. As a famous, old-time American magician called Al Baker once said, 'Why run if nobody's chasing you?'

We've written at some length here because, somewhere in this book, we wanted to get you thinking about magic. It isn't just about knowing tricks, it's also about how you do them. To take the scissors in this trick, they're there for a reason but we make them work for us in another way. Give thought to every trick you do, not just the 'how' of tricks, but the 'why' and the 'what if?' and 'what shall I say?' and 'when and where shall I say it?' and 'what does it look like to them?' and is there a 'better way', is there a 'simpler way' that is just as good? Do try thinking about your magic and its presentation. We've suggested a presentation with string and straw. It is only a suggestion, it may not suit you; think about how you would like to present it and why. What we are touching on here are the real secrets of magic. It isn't easy to be a master of your craft, but persevere and you, too, could be a magician! When you watch the *Paul Daniels Magic Show* on television remember that, once upon a time, Paul Daniels knew no more or no less about magic than you do now. He was a beginner, just like you. Think about it!

Even experts start as beginners.

9

Six Exclusive Sealed Mysteries

Up to now all the props for the tricks in the book you have been able to find at home or at school. But because we want you to become a super magician we have provided six custom-made exclusive sealed tricks in coloured envelopes which you can carry around with you, so you will never ever be stuck for something to do when asked. Read this chapter and master the secrets of the Six Sealed Mysteries.

The New Mysterious Magic-Age Cards

One question that Paul Daniels (that's me) is frequently asked, is, 'What was the first trick you ever learnt?' The answer to that is the Magic-Age Cards trick, except that we have made some changes to it that we think make it even more mysterious than it was before. It is one of the best small tricks of all time. I must have performed this trick thousands of times over the years, and provided you present it snappily, don't drag it out, you'll perform it thousands of times too.

You'll find the mysterious Magic-Age-Cards in the yellow envelope.

EFFECT

The magician displays seven small rectangular cards; each is covered with different groups of numbers on one side, and the words, 'Think of a Number', on the other. The magician claims that, with these mysterious magic cards, he can divine the number someone is thinking of, he can discover the number of the house, or flat, they live in if it's between 1 and 100, he can even discover the secret of how old they are! And the truth is he can, and he does!

SECRET

In the standard presentation six rectangular cards were used, all the same size and colour. The magician would ask a spectator to think of his age, he would then hand him all six cards with the instruction to hand back to him only those cards that had his age on them. If, for example, the spectator was twenty-five years old he would hand the magician the three cards that had the number 25 on each of them. The magician would glance at the groups of numbers and announce the spectator's age. A very good trick.

In our updated version the magician asks a spectator to think of any number that may be important to him: a birthday, a lucky number (between 1 and 100), a house number, etc. Whatever his choice, he must keep the number to himself. The magician hands him seven small cards; each has different groupings of numbers on its face. He is told to study the cards and to place any card on which his number appears face down on the table (we will use the number 47 as our example). The spectator places five cards face down on the table, the magician moves them, still face down, into the shape of a cross, holds his hands just above them for a few seconds as he concentrates, then announces, 'You are thinking of the number 47!'

This example is just one way of presenting this super effect. To understand how it works lay the cards out on the table face up and look at the smallest number on each card; it will always be in the top left-hand corner of each card. You will see that these numbers are in a progressive order. They are the key numbers which you must remember:

1,2,4,8,16,32,64. Here's an example of how it works. If you think of the number 40, pick up the cards that have 40 printed on them, and add the top left hand (or top) smallest numbers together, 8 + 32 = 40. That's it. That's the whole secret. All you ever do is silently add up the smallest numbers on the cards you are given; you already know where to look.

The improvement we have made is that, with a little practice, you can tell what the smallest number is on each card, without even having to look at the faces. The reason is that the backs of the cards are marked with tiny variations in the lettering which tell you what the number is. *You* can see it, but nobody else can because they don't know what to look for. The marking system is clearly explained on the eighth card of your set, and this is your Code Card.

This gives you more flexibility in presentation; you might do it once the standard way, then repeat it with the face-down lay-out.

A further variation in presentation is to ask the spectator to hold each card with his number on against his forehead. The reason for this is so the magician can tune into his thought waves. You won't be able to see the numbers because the backs of the cards will be facing outwards, but you can read the secret markings. Easy peasy for a sneaky magician.

If you practise learning the key card numbers, by sighting the markings on the backs and adding up the key numbers of different combinations of cards for ten minutes every day for two weeks, before you know it you will be able to do it in your sleep.

The Magic Coloured Boomerangs

In the green envelope is a very puzzling magic trick which is based on a purely optical illusion.

Effect

The magician exhibits two 'magic boomerangs', saying, 'You don't throw these about, you just stretch one so that it is longer than the other one, then you pick up the shorter one and stretch it so that it is now longer than the longer one which is now the shorter one. But, if you pick up the shorter one (which was longer) and stretch it, then it becomes longer again, not longer than it was, but longer than the longer one which is now the short one. Except, when you pick up the short one and turn it over, it becomes the long one. But, if you pick up the short one and turn it over and stretch it and put it on top of the long one, they both become the same size which is the right size to go in my pocket.'

Secret

To make sense of the presentation you will need to play with the boomerangs as I shall explain. What we have added to the Effect is to have four coloured sides, green and red for one boomerang and yellow and blue for the other, which makes it that little bit different from the norm.

Run through the following, with the boomerangs, and you will easily understand the principle. Then try it again, matching the patter (given under the Effect) to your actions and you will have added another super trick to your armoury of magic.

Put one of your boomerangs on the table, then put the other one underneath it so that the left short edge is in line with the one above it. You will then see that one of

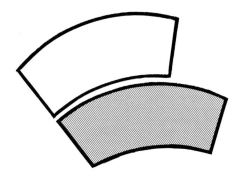

your boomerangs is larger than the other – really quite strange, isn't it? Pick up the smaller one, hold it between your hands and pretend to stretch it. Then put it back on the table below the other one and you will see that this one now looks larger than the other one. You can do it again, pick up the smaller one, pretend to stretch it by pulling, then put it below the one on the table (remember to make sure the left short edge is in line with the one above it). You will see that it looks larger than the other one. And you can do this again, and again, and again. But, of course, the really curious thing about it is that both boomerangs are exactly the same size. It is just a paradoxical, optical illusion. The way you line them up is what creates the effect and the business of pretending to stretch one is, of course, just business. It is a very unusual effect to carry in your pocket. Don't over-do it. Just perform it two or three times, then move on to your next trick. Have fun!

*H*orse *R*iders

Although, basically, a very fine puzzle (rather than magic), we think this is worth including in this book because we believe that the moment you solve a puzzle all by yourself, with no outside help, is a magic moment. You have achieved something and it's a very satisfying feeling – something you should pass on to your friends.

Many magicians love to solve puzzles, the process is not dissimilar to problem-solving in magic. And this particular puzzle is a classic; it was created over ninety years ago by the American puzzle king, Sam Loyd. You'll find it in the blue envelope.

*E*FFECT

The object of the puzzle is to place both riders on a horse, in the normal riding position, without folding, or cutting, or bending any of the three cards. They must be assembled flat on the table. Can you diddle it?

*S*ECRET

If you haven't worked it out already you will appreciate how subtle the solution is by looking at the final photo, which clearly shows how to solve the puzzle.

The Magic Domino Prediction

In the pink envelope is a wonderful presentation and a brilliant trick.

Effect

The magician turns his back on the audience while a spectator mixes up ten magic dominoes face down on the table. He then turns round and states that he is going to predict the random outcome of a game of dominoes played by the spectator. He moves one hand mysteriously over the face-down dominoes and, settling on one, picks it up and places it aside, face down. 'That is my prediction of something that will happen in the very near future,' he states emphatically.

'Please pick up all the dominoes and hold them face down in your hand. Now, I want you to play the game in the following way. Turn any domino face up on the table to start the game. Turn over a second domino and see if you can make a match; if one of the pictures matches either end of the domino on the table, then play it by butting the ends together. If you can't make a match, leave it face up on the

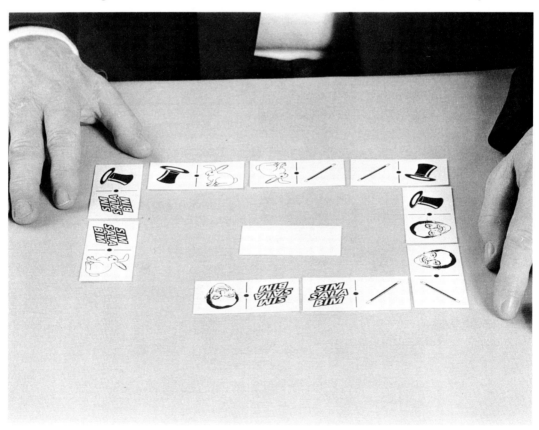

table and turn over the next domino. If that one's a match play it and then see if you can now match the other face-up domino before turning over any more. Carry on playing the dominoes, but always stick to this rule.'

The spectator should be able to form a progressive line in a rough rectangle shape. At the end of the game he will not be able to come to a conclusion, there will be unmatching pictures at the ends of each line. Occasionally, the spectator will end a game with the same picture on the end of each line. To avoid this you allow him to move the end domino of one line across, as a match, to the end domino of the other line.

Whichever way he arrives at the end of the game, the scene is set for you to turn your prediction domino face up to show that only this domino will close the game; it matches the end pictures of the dominoes at the end of each line.

SECRET

It works itself every time because ten dominoes form a closed loop. Removing one (as a prediction) and leaving nine dominoes means that the loop can only be closed by the tenth domino. So the magician always controls the outcome. This is a super secret, so keep it to yourself and don't risk exposing it by performing it more than once for the same audience.

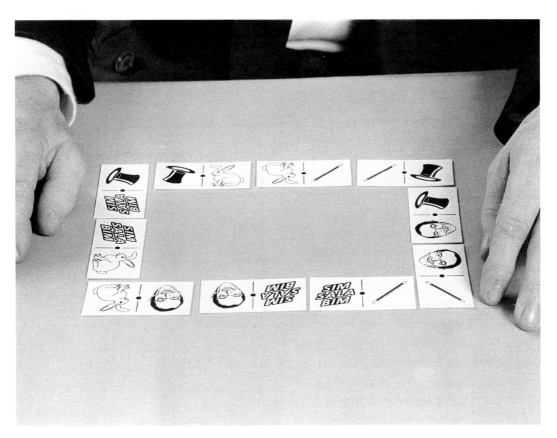

The Amazing Magic Playing-Card Calculator

The orange envelope contains the world's most inexpensive pocket calculator and will enable you to achieve a surprising prediction.

Effect

The magician shows the Amazing Magic Playing-Card Calculator to a friend and explains that this calculator, unlike all other calculators, actually reads minds. To demonstrate this he asks his friend to stick his left thumb up. The magician puts the calculator on the thumb.

'That has switched it on,' he explains. 'Now I want you to think of any number from 5 to 20 (which can include number 5 and number 20). Don't say the number aloud, just keep it in your mind. Now put your four fingers into the calculator in the digital assembly points provided (see photo 1). OK, done that? Now, starting with your index finger which you count as 1, the next finger as 2 (see photo 2), third finger as 3 (see photo 3) and little finger as 4, the first playing card as 5, the next card (counting clockwise) as 6 and so on, count out your chosen number as you go. When you have reached your

1

2

3

number, stop, then, counting the playing card you have stopped on as 1, the next as 2, and so on, start counting in reverse order (which means anticlockwise), tapping each successive playing card as you go. Don't go back up the fingers when

4

counting anticlockwise, stay on the cards. When you reach the number you are thinking of, stop (*see photo 4*). Look at the card you have stopped on. Now take your fingers out of the calculator and turn it over. Amazing!

SECRET

The effect works automatically; provided the counting is done as described the result will always be the same. To help you remember it, here's an example. We'll mentally select the number 12. So, counting the index finger as 1, second finger as 2, third as 3, little finger as 4, Ace of Spades as 5, 6 of Hearts as 6, 4 of Clubs as 7, 2 of Diamonds as 8, 3 of Spades as 9, Joker as 10, Ace of Hearts as 11, we reach the 5 of Diamonds as 12. We repeat the count in reverse order, counting (anticlockwise) the 5 of Diamonds as 1, Ace of Hearts as 2,

Joker as 3, 3 of Spades as 4, 2 of Diamonds as 5, 4 of Clubs as 6, 6 of Hearts as 7, Ace of Spades as 8, 9 of Diamonds as 9, 2 of Clubs as 10, 5 of Diamonds as 11 and Ace of Hearts as 12, our mentally selected number. Now turn the calculator over and you will see it has predicted the Ace of

5

Hearts (*see photo 5*). And that is all there is to it!

One word of caution; only ever show this trick once to the same person! You can make up your own versions of this, replacing playing cards with words or pictures. Whatever you use, the item to be predicted will always be in the position occupied, in our example, by the Ace of Hearts.

One last thought is not to have the prediction on the back of the calculator at all. Write it on a piece of paper instead, fold it up and tuck it into the spectator's top pocket, perform the trick as explained then let him open your prediction himself. A strong effect! This presentation is best achieved by using the second calculator we have provided, which has an animal theme. The animals listed are lion, horse, bear, rhino, cat, dog, rabbit, zebra, cow and Paul Daniels.

The Vanishing Rabbit

Magicians are famous for producing rabbits out of top hats. In the red envelope is an intriguing trick in which a magician makes a rabbit vanish into thin air.

Effect

Three pieces of card are laid out to form a picture that shows five rabbits wearing top hats plus another rabbit without a hat. Two pieces of card are changed round to make a picture that shows five rabbits wearing top hats; the other rabbit has vanished!

Secret

Assemble the three pieces of card in the following order: A and B over C; you will count five rabbits wearing hats and a sixth rabbit without a hat.

Now transpose pieces A and B to form a layout that reads B and A over C. Count the rabbits again and the sixth one has vanished. How, and where to?

Well, by exchanging pieces A and B you answer the 'how'. But where to? That's a horse of a different colour, as they say. It has something to do with the displacement of space and that is a deep, and mysterious, subject all by itself. All you need to know is that here is a perfect little mystery to carry in your pocket.